FROM THE CRESCENT TO THE CROSS

My Extraordinary Journey
to the Heart of God

SISTER MARYAMA

Published by Maryama Burger
California, U.S.A.
Printed in the U.S.A.

Cover design and interior layout by www.PearCreative.ca

ISBN: 978-0-9863166-0-9

I dedicate this book to the One I love,
who always reminds me to lose my rights
for the sake of love.

CONTENTS

Foreword by Cheryl Brodersen   7

Introduction   11

Acknowledgments   17

Part 1: God in the Shadows

1. Under the African Sky   21

2. Conflict and Uncertainty   29

3. Life in America—Temporary Insanity   37

4. Mourning and Despair—Yet with a Glimmer of Hope   47

5. The Cross in View   59

Part 2: The Light of the Cross

6. Seeking God, Finding Jesus   71

7. Strengthened to Stand in the New Life   79

8. Burdened by Legalism   89

9. The Key to Victory: My Life, Jesus' Life   99

10. Learning Freedom and Simplicity in Jesus   109

11. Meeting My Soul Mate   119

Part 3: Shining in a Dark World

12. Trials of Life   133

13. The Christian Paradox: Losing Everything, Having All   143

14. Suffering and Forgiving   153

15. New Opportunities to Serve   163

16. Rejoicing in Jesus in Every Season   173

Afterword: Channels of His Love   185

FOREWORD

Cheryl Brodersen

I first met Maryama at a Sunday evening through-the-Bible study taught by my father, Chuck Smith. Immediately I was drawn to Maryama's passion for God's Word and her love for the Lord. She spoke very kindly to me about my father and how she loved him as her pastor. She and her husband both regularly attended the service, so I saw Maryama quite frequently.

I was curious about Maryama. I wasn't quite sure of the origin of her accent, though her English was impeccable. One night, as we chatted after church, she told me that she was from Somalia and had grown up as a Muslim. Immediately I was curious. How had Maryama heard about Jesus? What had made her give her life to Jesus? By what means had she been brought to the United States?

As our friendship grew and our chats increased, I began to learn the answers to my questions. The answers were far more intriguing than I had imagined. Each time we talked, I wanted to know more about Maryama's background and how she came to be so passionate about Jesus.

About four years ago, I was invited to host an Internet talk show called *Today's Faith*. On each show I interviewed women and listened to their stories of how they came to faith and what God was doing in their lives. I knew that I wanted to have Maryama as one of my guests.

Her interview was fascinating. However, our time was limited, and we were only able to cover an incredibly small portion of Maryama's amazing journey. There was so much more of her story to be told.

Then one day Maryama informed me that the hospice company that she had been working for no longer wanted a chaplain to comfort their terminal patients. She was grieved for the loss of the opportunity to share the hope of heaven and salvation through Jesus more than the loss of a job. However, at the same time, she was feeling this internal conviction that she was to write her story. I almost jumped for joy out of my seat! "Yes!" I responded, perhaps a bit too enthusiastically. "If anyone has a story that needs to be written, it is you."

At that meeting I promised to introduce Maryama to an editor that I knew, Becky English. I knew that both women would be attending a leadership retreat hosted by Calvary Chapel Costa Mesa. I planned on introducing them there.

Upon arriving at the retreat, I made inquiries as to what room Becky was in. Imagine my surprise and delight when

I found out that these two women had been assigned to the same room as roommates! They had never met before, and Becky had not had any idea that I had suggested her name to Maryama.

I think it is important for every Christian woman to read Maryama's story. Too often we as Christians fail to understand how a person could love the Islamic faith. In our lapse we fail to show the necessary sensitivity to those under the bondage of Islam. By understanding why Muslims adhere to their faith, we are better able to present to them the true gospel of salvation through Jesus Christ.

Maryama, for me, also removed the veil of fear in presenting the gospel to a Muslim. She gave me a whole new perspective and enthusiasm for sharing the gospel with Muslim women.

I had the privilege of reading the first few chapters of Maryama's first draft. Honestly, I didn't want to stop there. I couldn't wait to read the rest of the book.

I pray that God will open your heart and mind to know the power of God to reach, transform, and use a beautiful Somali woman for His infinite glory. As you read Maryama's story, I pray that you will be inspired to surrender your own life to God's powerful purposes so that He can use you to share the glorious transforming gospel of Jesus Christ with a dying world.

Knowing Maryama's story has only endeared her further to my own heart. I am privileged to call her both sister and friend. I think that you will feel the same way when you read her story.

INTRODUCTION

You will seek Me and find Me,
when you search for Me with all your heart.
Jeremiah 29:13

In late 2013 I visited a sister of mine who is a great woman of God to seek some godly wisdom from her. As Cheryl and I communed with each other and our Jesus in the middle, my thoughts and words went to an evening in springtime in Somalia, my former country.

I could smell the evening with all its fragrances: the well-fed ground after the rain, the sheep, the goats with their young in the stalls, the camels and cattle in their places. We were well fed, and my brothers and sisters and extended cousins pulled out our camp beds under the beautiful African sky. As we lay on our mats, talking and giggling, I noticed the glorious sky, with billions and billions of stars glittering in the vast expanse and shooting stars everywhere.

This is one of the many times that the thought of God entered my mind, but with it was an awesome fear. I trembled a little because of the massiveness of the sky with its shooting stars crossing all over the heavens. For a moment I thought war was going on in the heavens.

Just then one of my cousins called to me, and my thoughts of God were left for another day . . .

* * * * *

I had come to see Cheryl Brodersen, the wife of Brian, one of our pastors, because I had recently lost my job. I had been a chaplain for a hospice company, and I had ministered to dying people and their families to comfort them, encourage them, and give them hope. That was my job, and to give them anything less than God was to me a cruel thing to do.

A week before my termination, the supervisor of patient care told me that dying people do not want to hear about Jesus. I was written up and told that I must not do this any longer. I was stunned and felt sick to my stomach. Something deep within, or shall I say Someone, told me that my days of being a chaplain were coming to an end.

Sure enough, a week later I was let go. I did not protest, because I knew that God had allowed it and therefore it must be okay. But the hurt was there, and it would take time to heal.

That day I heard in my spirit God telling me to write my story. I was not sure if it was really God, so I did what a believer is expected to do—I inquired of the Lord by sharing what was in my heart with close Christian sisters who were mature in the faith. Some asked if I had experience writing, to which I answered no, and some suggested that I research how to write a book. I began to doubt.

Then I sensed the Lord's voice. He said, "Go and see Cheryl Brodersen."

I said, "Oh Lord, Cheryl just lost her father" (my pastor, Chuck Smith). "I should be comforting her and not burdening her." But the Holy Spirit reassured me that it was okay. He practically dragged me to Cheryl.

She seemed happy to see me, and after we caught up and I told her about my woes, I shared what I thought God was telling me. Cheryl was elated. She told me that it was from God and said that my testimony needed to be told. My question was, "How do I start? I have never written a book before, and English is my second language." I will never forget what she said: "Start with the African skies you told me about."

* * * * *

Suddenly I knew that this book would be about the human soul searching for safe harbor and about God's relentless pursuit to restore humanity to our original state, when we had sweet fellowship with Him in the evening (see Genesis 3:8).

I began searching for God, or at least wondering about Him, as a Muslim shepherd girl in Somalia. My restless search took me far from my country, far from my family, and far from my religion. I eventually landed in the United States with its mind-blowing philosophies of individualism, self-gratification, and liberal feminism.

When I first came to the U.S., I did not work; instead I had the privilege of watching Sesame Street with my daughter. It was a novelty for both of us. Perhaps it would have been therapeutic for me to work and avoid the world of soap opera, as it was truly damaging to my soul and gave me a wrong understanding of American culture.

Americans assumed that I should be thankful to be in this country, and I was, because I was experiencing for the first time freedom of religion and thought, and that was huge. But at the same time I longed to belong; I wished to be in a place where everybody knew my name.

I'm not sure why I ended up in the U.S. Was it because two American kids had to come through me to make America beautiful? Was it because twenty-three of my Somali family members who would have perished otherwise would find safe haven in this land? Or was it to bring Ken's wife, friend, and sister here? Perhaps I was a missing part of the body of Christ in this country, or perhaps my American sisters were missing me and I them. The reasons are endless, but each of them was part of God's plan.

I finally found a place to belong when I came to know Jesus. I was born into a living organism—the body of Christ. But I went through a great deal of trial, confusion, and hardship before I got there. In this area the church has a great opportunity. I wish someone would have mentored me or at least told me that what I was seeing on television was not what was a real representation of the country. Maybe someday the church will have a place for the newcomers, and may it begin with me.

* * * * *

I came to know Jesus when I really looked at a cross for the first time and asked someone what it meant. I was told the story of the Bible, which is really the story of Jesus, and I came to understand that Jesus had died on the cross to pay for my sin and the sin of all people. I fell in love with Him that day. Since then I have sought to know Him, my Shepherd, more and more. I have found Him in His Word and in His Spirit and also in His people.

I wrote this book to share my Jesus with those who are searching. I have learned that there are three kinds of people in the world, and it is to each of these groups that I address my story.

First, many of you already know Jesus and embrace who He is. You have accepted with a thankful heart what He has done on your behalf. To this group I say, blessed are you. Enjoy your God as He enjoys you.

Second are carnal Christians—those of you who have heard, seen, and tasted the Lord and yet do not possess Him. You either think that you must do something to deserve His amazing love, or else the world has a grip on you, making you afraid simply to trust Him fully. To you I say, choose today whom you are going to serve (see Joshua 24:15). God will not share His glory with anyone. He loves you, and He will be enough for you if you don't add anything to Him.

And third are unbelievers. If you do not believe in Jesus, you are missing Him. How do I know? Because you are full of worry, fear, anger, and unforgiveness. You are trying to control your world that is unraveling around the edges. You collect stuff, yet you don't enjoy it. Life means living for today, and yet you don't have zest for life. You lack clarity—you think you know, and yet you don't. You are always searching for the next best thing and yet not finding it.

Believe me, I know, because I have been there. But if you don't believe me, read the book of Ecclesiastes, and you will find yourself there. God is saying to you, "Come now, and let us reason together" (Isaiah 1:18), and, "Come to Me, all you who labor and are heavy laden, and I will give you rest" (Matthew 11:28). You have tried everything else—why not try God? I pray that you will, for He is the only One who can satisfy.

This book is a call to the ardent follower of Jesus to be encouraged, to the carnal man to be committed to the upward call, and to the unbelieving man to come home. May you read this book with spiritual eyes and understand it with a spiritual mind.

ACKNOWLEDGMENTS

I give thanks to the Lord Jesus Christ, who lifted me up from darkness into His marvelous light and who, when the time was just right, used my inclination and personality to birth this book.

I am also forever grateful for all the people He has brought into my life to make this book a reality for His glory.

The leader of the band is my beloved husband, Ken, who happens to be my brother in Christ and an unforgettable friend. Thank you for your grace, mercy, and patience, which you show me every day. You always make me look good, love.

Cheryl Brodersen's guidance, wisdom, discernment, and encouragement have made this book happen. I give thanks to our Lord every time I think of you. I love you, sister. Thank you for what you mean to me and to the body of Christ. You sure are your father's daughter.

To Rebecca English, my editor—and not just an editor but a beloved sister whose knowledge, spiritual insight, and integrity have made this book look good—thank you, Becky.

I am grateful for Patty Chavez, who helped type the first draft of this book. Thank you, Patty.

I give my heartfelt thanks to Yvonne Parks, who designed the cover and the interior of the book and was able to listen to my desires, and also to Jennifer Cullis for proofreading the manuscript and to Jason Chatraw for creating the e-book. Your contributions to this book are immeasurable. Thank you.

I am thankful for my kids, Eda and Eric. My love for them kept me in this country, where I met the greatest love of all, *Jesus*. But it is normal for me to say that I have six kids: Matthew, my husband's son, is married to Jen. Eda belongs to Jeremy, and Sally belongs to Eric. Now Matthew and Jen have given us a beautiful granddaughter, Heather, and another is on the way. Who would have thought that a little Somali shepherdess would one day have a family that represents different peoples, tongues, and tribes from Africa, North America, and Europe? Only God. It is no secret that He has blessed me immensely. I love you, kids, and my thoughts of you always warm my heart.

Lastly, I thank all the friends and beloved sisters whom God has brought into my life and who have loved me unconditionally. I in return love you. Thank you all; you make my life better.

PART 1

GOD
IN THE
SHADOWS

1

UNDER THE AFRICAN SKY

The heavens declare the glory of God.
Psalm 19:1

As a Muslim child, I really did not know much about God personally. But I could see Him in His beautiful creation.

Springtime in northern Somalia has always been precious to me. In Africa water is life, and when the early rain comes, it looks as if the earth has put on its best dress. The wind dances, the people sing, and the animals play. Everything seems in its place in that season—the earth that has been groaning due to lack of rain is satisfied, and it happily yields its vegetation, herbs, and fruits. People are satisfied too, as are the animals.

In the springtime, when schools were closed, my dad always sent my brothers and sister and me to his house in the countryside. It was my happiest time, because that is when I saw the awesome glory of God in the stars, in the moon, in the animals, and in the trees, flowers, and vegetation. Everything resounded the Creator's pleasure in His creation.

I wondered at the awesomeness of it all and longed to know the Creator.

I knew that God was the Creator of all things and that He desired us to do good. I knew that one day He would judge the world, or, even sooner, He would judge us when we died. I knew too that He was holy and required us to be holy inside and out. Outside holiness was attainable through the five pillars of Islam:

1. God is one, and God's final and favorite prophet was Mohammed.
2. We were supposed to pray five times a day facing Mecca through rituals of washing in methodical fashion.
3. We had to fast one month of the year from dawn to dusk.
4. We had to give alms, about 2 percent of what we had.
5. We were supposed to visit Mecca once in our lifetime if financially possible.

If we followed all the rules of Islam, we had a chance with God and were considered good Muslims. Even so, all rights were reserved for God to do with us what He pleased. I never heard that God loved me or that He was even capable of loving. A relationship with God was not mentioned in Islam.

In Islam there is no way of knowing God; a Muslim must just try to follow these rituals and hope for the best and fall on God's mercy.

The Ten Commandments were part of my understanding of Islam except the command to keep the Sabbath, as Muslims rest on Friday. Heaven and hell are well understood in Islam: if you are good, you go to heaven; if you are bad, you go to hell. Who decides whether one is good or bad? God does—end of story. So people are left not knowing what will become of them when they die.

I grew up fearing God, which is not a bad thing, in a sense. I saw the glorious splendor of His majestic creation and saw also His fearsome acts in floods, droughts, and death. But I did not know Him.

* * * * *

My father was born around 1914—nobody knows exactly when. Thirty years or so before he was born, in 1884, the African continent was divided into multiple territories by European invaders. My grandfather was a member of the guerillas who fought, beginning in 1899, against British occupation. The war between Somalia and Great Britain lasted about twenty-one years, and England finally defeated the Somalis through air bombings. My grandfather died in the fight, and the family lost everything. My grandmother and her two young boys became beggars, because the British took their livestock to punish the Somalis for fighting against them. Sheep, goats, horses, camels—all gone. This was the plight of all Somalis in the northern region; they suffered much. So Somalia became occupied by the British.

My grandmother and her two young sons wandered around and were able to acquire a few goats and sheep from relatives. Thus they survived. One night a lion attacked them and took my father by the head and almost crushed him, but my brave grandmother ran after the lion with a great log of fire, and the lion dropped the boy, who was left for dead. But Grandma nursed him. She put him on a donkey and headed for a clinic, and two days later they arrived. The left side of my father's head and his left eye were crushed, and the English couple who ran the clinic asked my grandmother to leave him behind if he was going to have a chance to survive. So my grandmother left her son behind, and that was the last time my father saw his mother.

My father grew up in the English compound. He learned to read and write, and eventually he acquired a medical profession. Even though he had only one eye, he grew up strong, dark, and handsome, with all the etiquette of an English gentleman. God blessed him with land and houses and much livestock—hundreds of sheep, goats, camels, and other animals—and he hired his family clan to manage it all for him. Even though my father suffered some deformity, he was, as I mentioned, tall, dark, and handsome, and he was also rich. The rich part made him a good catch.

My father married his first wife, my aunt, and she died within six months of a mysterious illness. My dad mourned for her with the rest of the family, but soon he was ready to marry my second aunt, as it was the custom of the culture.

Also, since Father was a man of substance, it was good for the survival of the family and the clan for him to remarry. But two years later death struck again, and my second aunt died giving birth to her second son. Another loss for Father and the family. But now my father's firstborn, Mohamoud, had arrived. Once again he was a widower, this time with a young child. What was the family to do? Give him the last daughter—my mom.

Dad was comforted by my mom, who loved him in spite of his deformities. And she was loved by him. Many times people heard him say, "She gave me life and taught me how to love and live." Mother bore him five children: her firstborn, Ahamed; my sister, Anab; me; my younger brother, Mohammed; and an infant that died. She also raised Father's firstborn, Mohamoud, from my aunt.

My four siblings moved with my mom and dad to the city, but my grandmother, who stayed behind in the country to manage my father's livestock with my uncles, desired to keep me. Since I was a middle child and the second daughter, Mom and Dad thought they would not miss me much. After all, Dad had his three boys, and Mom had her girl. What I did not know was that Someone else had His eyes on me, and He had to raise me in the fields where the sheep, goats, camels, oxen, and cattle were on the open beautiful African savannah, where the earth teemed with life and the sky displayed His glory, where the rain of His tears fed the earth and His thunder revealed His displeasure with a world that was out of tune with Him.

Even as a young child, I was aware of Him in His creation, and I felt His presence at times. But although He knew me,

I did not know Him. My grandmother taught me how to care for the baby sheep and lambs. I was fond of them; they were my favorite pets. Each one was special and had its own name, and even though sheep and goats and other animals look the same to untrained and uncaring eyes, I knew each of my sheep by name. If one was missing, I knew exactly which one. Remind you of Someone?

Looking back, I realize how fortunate I was, for I learned to love and enjoy the wonder of His creation. I always thought that I was special. I was the overseer of the livestock and a good helper to my grandmother. This was affirmed by my family, and I truly believed it. I am thankful for that, because there is nothing worse for a child's feelings than not being wanted. I was a dreamer, and I ran and played in the fields with lots of imagination. Come to think of it, I wonder what was real and what was imagined in my young mind. But I am grateful for it all.

* * * * *

When I was five, death visited our family again. This time it was my mom, my beloved mom! It was the spring of 1962. I clearly remember the day my mom died. It rained seven days continuously after that as if the sky was crying for my mom. Still today people remember that spring and call it the time the sky was opened. The ground was covered with all kinds of flowers, also berries and caterpillars. Even today I am fearful of caterpillars.

My dad was in Russia for school, and my mom had been dealing with some sort of illness. Later on it was understood to be ovarian cancer. It was my first loss. Even though I did not understand the details, my grandmother's wailing told me that something awful had happened.

I truly thought my mom would appear again, and it took me a long time to realize that death was final. She left broken hearts and shattered lives everywhere—my poor dad; my grandmother, who had lost her last daughter; my mom's relatives. Everybody lost, for my mom was a truly beautiful, kind, and generous person, and she was truly beloved. But of all those, none mourned more for my mom than my poor dad. People still say today that my dad died with my mom and was a shell after her death. Life went on with our broken hearts, and from then on I understood that death was my enemy.

After my mom's death Father took my grandmother and me with him to the city. It was then that I started my schooling. We all went to boarding school, where well-to-do Africans send their kids. I hated it. It was too much for a young shepherdess to have to be trained in snobbery in a world of pretense and showoffs and schedules, routines, and properness. All vanity.

At school I had a trunk in which to put all my belongings. It had a lock and a key, and my dad had instructed my sister and me not to lose the keys. But by the end of the term, the keys were lost, along with my clothes and my shoes. The servants informed my dad that the trunk was empty and had no keys or lock, and my dad said, "Another year, and she will be mindful of her things." Sure enough, as I grew, there came a day when I came home with my trunk full of clothes and shoes and with my keys. I am thankful for Dad's kindness and grace. He was more interested in my maturity than the stuff I was losing.

Springtime, when school closed, was a special time. It was then that I could get relief from the world of boarding school. We were off to the country, and I connected with my familiar place. I loved the sights and sounds of the animals, trees, rain, stars. But now the death of my mom had seared my soul, and I became conscious of death, even though the beauty of spring was evident everywhere I looked. There was a shadow of death looming, and at times I was pretty sure that I saw a tall, dark figure with no face around me. It was fearsome. I had heard stories about death and how he loomed around us until our time came, so in my young mind he became real to me, and I would ask Allah to protect me from him.

I often wondered what happens to us when we die, so I asked my grandmother one day. Her answer brought me grief and helplessness, because she stated, "God will judge what we have done, good or bad, and He also will judge our hearts and our thoughts." As I grew up, I came to understand that I must try my best to appease this God who seemed unappeasable.

2

CONFLICT AND UNCERTAINTY

*The way of peace they have not known,
and there is no justice in their ways; they
have made themselves crooked paths; whoever
takes that way shall not know peace.
Isaiah 59:8*

My siblings and I became busy with our lives. Dad was an empty shell and did the routines of life without much joy. Even though Dad was not an affectionate man, he was loyal and trustworthy, a protector, a good provider. He was known in the city and in most of the country, and we enjoyed the privilege of being his kids and found great favor among the people because of it. He always believed in us, and we had a sense of safety and assurance because he was our father. He loved us tangibly.

Grandma was lost in her grief, but she was always there for us. Her tender care and wisdom and strength were immeasurable, especially for me. She was my anchor. I remember always falling asleep in her lap. I did this until the age of fourteen, when one day a boy made fun of me. That ended my sleeping in my grandma's lap.

After the death of my mom, Dad was done with marriages and determined to be a widower. But the tribe would not have it. Six years after my mom's death, a girl, my mother's second niece, was coming of age, and the family offered her to my dad. After all, the wealth had to remain in the family, because the family took care of the livestock. So my dad took his fourth wife.

Unfortunately, my father's marriage did not favor me or my siblings. My father's new wife did not care about us. Perhaps she knew how much my father had loved my mom and saw us as the reflection of that love. She was determined to separate us from our father, so the family became divided and contentious. Bitterness and all kinds of ugly emotions became part of our lives. When Dad withdrew from us and we were not the center of his love anymore, every one of the siblings handled it differently. We never really talked about it. I learned to hang on in quiet desperation.

During that time I withdrew and showed no interest in my family's life. There was no love and certainly no faith. But still there was hope, and how thankful I was for that hope.

* * * * *

My teen years were spent in boarding school. Dad always sent the Land Rover with a driver to pick us up for the weekends, but I always asked my dad if I could walk home with my friends, and once in a while I had the chance. Seeing Grandma was always comforting, and it made visiting our gloomy house bearable.

I began to like boarding school and got into fashion and dresses and shoes. I even received a letter or two from secret admirers. My sister was more social than I was, but I managed to have a few tea parties of my own. Still, I wished sometimes that I could take a walk in the field, but that was not cool for city girls. This was the beginning of the end of this young shepherd girl.

I did not visit the countryside as often as I would have liked, because my stepmom went instead. Dad stayed in the city when she went, and he had us all to himself and could love us once again. He sacrificed two and half months without his wife so that we could all enjoy each other with Grandma. Dad talked to us about Mom and reminded us of how wonderful our mom had been. It brought a little comfort but also sadness. It made me miss the mom I never had a chance to know. Death did this to me.

I managed to do well in school, and when I left at the age of sixteen, I was accepted in nursing school. I was betrothed to a young man who was a lieutenant in the military and planned to be married after nursing school.

I grew rapidly in nursing college. I lived in a beautiful hostel God provided for me, snug in the woods in a small hilly city in the north of Somalia, and was glad to be away from home, which was full of sadness and brokenness. It was a beautiful season in my life. My mind was expanding—I learned of human psychology and sociology, and I began to feast on humanistic ideology. Rapidly the thought of God was diminishing in my life; I was soon not aware of Him at all. Once in a while I saw a rainbow or a flower that reminded me that there was something bigger, but the thought always fled away.

The nursing school was run by UNICEF, a branch of the UN. Our teachers were Canadian and mostly European. I was taught to believe that religion was for ignorant people and that knowledge did not allow room for God. Whenever the students brought Him up, God was politely dismissed. We were not told that there was *no* God, since these educators were in a Muslim country, but in every area of life in that college, subtly and subliminally it was implied that God had no place or significance in our lives. Values clarification was the only menu, and the idea that truth was subjective was the order of the day.

Little by little my hedges were removed; everything I valued was dismantled, brick by brick. It made me uncomfortable, but it also relieved me to think that I didn't have to worry about God, who was hard to know anyway. But still He knew me.

After I graduated from nursing school, I decided that I did not want to marry the man I was betrothed to, and my betrothal was annulled. Since the Islamic religion recognizes betrothal as legally binding, I had to have a certificate of divorce, even though the marriage was not consummated. So there I was, divorced at the age of nineteen without having had any relations with the man.

Because I had been one of the top three in my class at graduation, I had been guaranteed a full scholarship to the

American University in Beirut, Lebanon. But civil war broke out, and the scholarship was canceled. Another setback. It seemed the end of the world for me.

* * * * *

During my years in nursing school, I had become increasingly numb toward God and toward life in Somalia. So many things were happening in my life that did not make sense at all, either to me or to my family. I felt some mixture of disappointment, disenchantment with life, maybe even outright rebellion. All my friends were content with marrying Somali men, but I was not. It seemed as if an irresistible force beckoned me to a distant land that I did not know.

One night I met an old American man at a social gathering. He was fifty-three and an engineer who traveled the world in his work, and he promised me a life in America. He was my ticket out of my present turmoil.

We were married in Alexandria, Egypt. Since I was a Muslim and he was not, he was compelled to convert to Islam by the Egyptian authorities if he wished to marry me. He complied—I guess his Christianity did not mean much to him. But there was a bigger plan.

We stayed in Egypt for a while after the wedding and then went to Saudi Arabia. My husband routinely signed six- to twelve-month contracts; when a job was done, we moved. It was nice to move around, for it satisfied my restless, nomadic life. Or perhaps, although I did not know it at the time, I was being given a well-rounded exposure to various cultures so that I could one day be planted in the body of Christ for holy use. In Saudi Arabia we had a beautiful villa with servants and all, and we enjoyed the secret decadent world of well-to-do Saudis. There my beautiful daughter, Eda, was born. She was the joy of our lives. She was a bright and beautiful baby, and I was blessed to be her mom.

Yet a deep sadness and longing filled my heart. I learned to fill it with stuff just as everyone else around me did, since my husband was well off, and I had stuff now. Deep thoughts about life, God, and grief were dampers; I was better off occupying myself with the here and now.

My relationship with my dad was getting worse. I had been rebellious, marrying an older man outside my faith and my culture—a man who was in my family's mind an infidel. Having peace with my dad was valuable to me. Even though I had brought him shame, I knew my dad loved me, and the thought that he did not approve of my life was painful. So when Eda was seven months old, I went back to Somalia to see my family. They were so glad to see me, especially my sister and my younger brother. Out of respect for my dad, I did not see him for a few days. I waited until he called for me, but I was determined to restore our relationship. The day I saw him, I took my beautiful seven-month-old daughter and put her in his lap and bowed down before him. He held my daughter in his bosom and stretched out his right hand and placed it on my head, and he kissed my daughter. I wept bitterly. I received the blessing of my daddy that day. After all the bad stuff I had done, I was forgiven.

Being in Somalia comforted me. I was reminded of the stability of my culture, my people, and my land. I saw my beautiful, spacious African sky, and once again the thought of the Creator was aroused within me, although it quickly passed.

After a few months my husband came to collect us, and we moved to the island of Bahrain, the playground of the Saudis, where they run to find reprieve from their restrictive, rigid lives of Islam. We resumed living with an abundance of stuff and were surrounded by American and European expats and wealthy locals. Once again I delved into a world of no lack. God, the Creator, was never mentioned, even among Muslims.

* * * * *

In August of 1980, one month before my daughter turned two, we moved to the U.S. I remember entering JFK Airport and witnessing the sea of humanity from all different tribes and tongues and with all shades of skin—so many people, so many languages. I felt lost. Then we entered New York City. It was a city on the go: everyone on a mission, no one turning left or right, each person moving straight forward as if their very lives depended on it. I wondered where they were all going. What was the rush?

The skyscrapers were awful to me—there was no sky in Manhattan. The Democratic Convention between Ted Kennedy and President Carter was going on while we were there. The city was festive—lots of noise, everybody trying to persuade each other and get their points across. It was interesting.

I had come to the U.S. once about a year earlier to get my citizenship papers started and had stayed about two weeks. I had gone to see a college football game between Yale

University and Penn State with friends of ours in Virginia, and I assumed that "football" meant soccer. I waited for the game to start; I thought that the actual football was the pre-game. When I asked my friend at halftime when the game was supposed to start, she was shocked to find out that I was waiting for a soccer game. Penn State won.

Those two weeks in the U.S. were intriguing. I was astonished at the beauty of the country. I found people open and kind. I liked their spirit of independence and open-mindedness and, believe it or not, their fairness. Their history of prejudice was not revealed to me, or, at least, I was not looking for it. When someone was rude, I always thought they were just having a bad day or a bad life, and I often apologized for them. People were puzzled by my attitude, but the thought of someone judging me because of my color was ludicrous to me. Judge me by my character or my ability or how I behave, but that I am dark tells you nothing about me.

Now, as I took in New York City with my family, I noticed that it was very cold. My husband told me that Southern California was Mediterranean, as it is in Somalia, so I said, "Let's go there!" We headed for California and settled in Huntington Beach.

3

LIFE IN AMERICA— TEMPORARY INSANITY

The fool has said in his heart, "There is no God." They are corrupt, they have done abominable works, there is none who does good.
Psalm 14:1

Life in America was good at first, but not for long. Americans thought that I should be thankful to be here, but I politely let them know that life in America was difficult and confusing. I had come from a culture of belonging, in which each person was his brother's keeper, and all of a sudden I was in the midst of a culture that was free in its thinking and encouraged a spirit of individualism. I became lost in this philosophy.

There was something enticing and freeing about this individualistic mind-set, but there was also something scary and unsettling about a life that was not accountable to anyone but oneself. It meant that people stood alone and fell alone. What a concept! Most disturbing of all was freedom of religion. People could believe anything they wanted, and nobody had the right to legislate their right to believe.

My last brick was dismantled, and I was left to myself. I felt alone and spiritually naked—no boundaries, no hedges around me. I felt awful, but there was no turning back from this life. It was full speed ahead.

* * * * *

I began to inquire as to what other people held sacred, and it was *self.* So I said in my heart, *I should explore self.* Sad to say, when I looked inside myself, I felt even more uncertainty, fear, and lack of control over my life and had no assurance of anything. Everything was vague; I had no clarity. I was incapable of navigating in life without a foundation. I truly felt disconnected from some definite source, whoever and whatever that was.

Counseling proved to be unprofitable. Self-esteem failed me miserably. I explored New Age thinking, to no avail. I tried horoscopes and psychic readings and came up empty handed.

A couple years after moving to the U.S., my marriage with my old American husband ended after a long struggle. Not long after we went our separate ways, I met the man who would be the father of my son. He loved me and Eda and wanted to marry me. I was not sure of marrying him but was happy to live with him, and as a result my beautiful son, Eric, was born in December of 1984. We almost lost him in a miscarriage, but God showed His mercy to us, although we neither thanked Him nor acknowledged His mercy. Soon after Eric was born, I came to the conclusion that his father was not for me.

Not thinking of my two children, Eda and Eric, my life continued to be full of confusion and many mistakes. It was life under the sun, as Ecclesiastes 2:17 describes it. All my endeavors at religion and self-esteem turned out to be fruitless.

Then came Scientology. It promised to solve my problems through a series of audits, which meant going back and erasing my childhood traumas. Ah! This might be the answer to the emptiness of my life. The auditors charged me a small fee, but the fees increased each week, each month. I was audited in order to erase my childhood traumas, but it brought more grief and disturbed emotions. The auditor was a strong, tall man, maybe in his forties, and he had a thumb or a finger missing. There was something sinister about him, and I would not let him penetrate my mind. I just kept thinking about his missing finger. I didn't know it, but God was my protection.

I continued with Scientology, the prices increasing each session with more books. I sold my gold jewelry to pay for it, hoping to find peace for my aching soul, and continued with lectures and one-on-one auditing.

One day in a lecture the instructor was teaching us how we would become thetan, or actually God. He said that as we progressed, we would experience self with no conflict, no past traumas, no wrongness at all—we would be like God. That was the ultimate purpose of Scientology.

Everybody was delighted to hear this, but oh, me! My last hope of having peace, meaning, and direction was dashed into pieces. Something within the depth of my soul was seared, and I realized that I was about to cross a line. I truly felt as if life was drained from me. Something in my soul convinced me that I was not God, neither could I be God. The thought of being equal with God made me sick to my stomach.

I left that evening and never went back. I had lost all my gold for nothing. But it was the providence of God.

Hypnosis was my last frontier, and it made me miserable. It seemed unholy and unsacred to let some stranger have access to my innermost being. Everybody I sought help from assumed that I was running from my past—that a deep secret, some awful thing that had happened to me, needed to be uncovered. But all I wanted to know was how to escape the death that would someday come upon me and how I could know the God who displayed His beauty and majesty upon the African skies. Was there any way of knowing Him?

* * * * *

I came to realize that there were no answers, so in order to save the little resources I had, I decided to become part of the masses, put on a freshly made mask, and fully embrace American individualism. I dejectedly accepted the "it's all about me" philosophy. My horizontal life continued as I focused on the things around me, and any thought of God diminished. My life was filled with activity, chatter, and worthless, even harmful, things—anything to shut out the still voice of God.

In 1986 I decided to take my two kids, now eight and two, to Somalia for a while that summer. Afterward I planned to move to Dubai, in the United Arab Emirates, where my license to practice nursing was valid. I schemed the plan to escape with the kids and never to come back to the U.S. But Eric's father realized that I did not love him enough to marry him and guessed that if I left the country with Eric I might not come back. So he refused to let me take my son. He persuaded me to take only Eda and then come back.

My visit to Somalia was comforting to me. I always felt grounded and balanced there. It is nice to be in a place where everybody knows your name. There is something about Africa that balances a person. I often thought that maybe it was because it is in the center of the earth or because the gravitational pull grounded one. Or perhaps it was just home.

During the time I was there, the country was shifting politically and culturally. People seemed different from what I remembered—dishonesty, lying, corruption, deception, and lack of trust were everywhere. Everybody was trying to use and manipulate others. I felt the land crying for justice and equity. The poor were oppressed, and I wept for them. I felt their suffering. God came to view once again, and I asked, "Does God know all this?" Questions with no answers flooded my mind again, and I was overwhelmed. Once again those thoughts were stuffed down, for it was the only way I could go on.

The visit was cut short because of the uncertainty in the country. Visiting with my family was nice, and I had a good time with my dad, my siblings, and my grandmother. I loved them, and I felt that this was the last time I would see them—especially my grandmother, who was advanced in age. We wept bitterly and kissed. Again death entered my mind, and I wondered about the possibility of seeing each other after death. I had not heard any such thing before, so sorrow filled my heart. Saying goodbye was tough.

Eda and I left for Dubai, reluctantly leaving my beloved Somalia behind. I did not get the chance to visit the countryside with my daughter to let her be a shepherdess for a while. My family insisted it was not safe with the country as it was. I was sad that I did not get the chance to hear, smell, and touch my beloved sheep. Eda would have loved it, and I would have been comforted.

In the wake of my disappointment, our stay in the Emirates was just what I needed. We delved into the abundance and luxury that the Emirates has to impart. Eda's father was in Dubai, and I had many friends there, and we connected and enjoyed each other. I explored the possibility of working as a registered nurse and found that it could be done. Eda's father enrolled Eda in a prestigious private school where diplomats and Europeans send their children. My daughter had a Mercedes with a chauffeur and lived in her father's penthouse on the tenth floor right at the beach, or the Cornish, as we call it. All this happened in a span of two months.

But even with all the benefits, two months seemed like two years. I missed my son. No life was worth living without my two kids by my side. Eda's father convinced me that it would be good for us to stay in Dubai because he could offer Eda a better life there, and it made sense, but I could not stay without my son. So I left Eda with her father and came to the United States, hoping that I could convince Eric's father to let me take Eric back with me. If not, I was willing to steal him if I had to.

My hope was to work and raise my two kids in the Emirates. It had a lot to offer—not least a beautiful, comfortable lifestyle with lots to distract a person from any spiritual thoughts. It was more cohesive than life in Southern California. Evening strolls and afternoon siestas were common. People were connected. Dubai was a dynamic city. Even though it was a place of wealth and luxury, people were more in tune with each other and more historically and culturally oriented; deep conversations were welcomed, which fostered a climate of connection. The Islamic and European cultures were somewhat compatible in the sense that each enjoyed deep-thinking conversations, and it seemed that most people who came there were the cream of the crop from different countries. The city nurtured a community of foreigners and locals who embraced the issues of life under the sun.

Dubai also had a vibrant Somali community. It boasted mostly educated Somalis—doctors, nurses, lawyers, business executives, and merchants—who had left the political climate of Somalia and found a sweet haven there. Dubai was a perfect fit for me. It was a beautiful international community of people who embraced each other.

No one asked me where I was from; I fit right in with the other Somalis there. It was good to know that I belonged. God was not in the minds of the people, and that was fine with me.

So I set out for the U.S., hoping to collect my son and return to the Emirates. But my plans were dashed once again when Eric's father refused to let his son go. I was back in the country whose lifestyle I had never adjusted to, and I was forced to stay because of my son. I missed my daughter in the Emirates; telephone bills mounted up. I insisted that Eda come back to be with me, for she missed her mom and brother. By the grace of God, Eda's father relented and let Eda come to the United States.

Her dad arranged for her to fly with the airline crew from Dubai to Holland to Los Angeles. When my daughter came toward me in the airport, carrying her backpack and with the captain holding her hand, she tried to run to me. But the captain would not let her go without checking my ID to be sure that I was indeed her mom.

* * * * *

So there I was in Southern California, not having much except both my kids. For the first time I resigned myself to staying in the U.S., and I decided to become a U.S. citizen. *If you can't beat them*, I reasoned, *join them*.

When I had been in Somalia, my beloved younger brother, Mohammed, had asked me if I would help him, as he was planning to come to the U.S. to study. I had agreed to help, but now that I found myself with two kids and no substance to speak of and busy with my fragmented life, I put away the plan to help him, hoping I would have a more opportune time.

Sadly, the opportunity never materialized. I went under the radar and broke all communications with my family back home, because I did not have the means to help anyone and was ashamed to admit it. Everyone in the U.S. was assumed by those in my home country to be wealthy, and since I had left my culture and chosen to marry outside my religion and tradition, no one would show any sympathy to me. I was sure that I would be judged and criticized if they found out I was poor and broken.

4

Mourning and Despair— Yet with a Glimmer of Hope

Blessed are those who mourn, for they shall be comforted.
Matthew 5:4

My grandmother passed when she was in her nineties. She had been through a lot in her life: she had buried eight children, her husband, and four grandchildren, including my older brother Mahamoud, who had been a major in the special forces in the Somali military. He had been killed in the war between Somalia and Ethiopia in 1978. It had been a great loss for our family, and we had mourned him for a long time.

Through all her suffering, my beloved grandmother had been strong and resilient yet gentle. She'd had great wisdom and insight. She had been a devout Muslim who worshiped the one God who had created her and everything else—she had been faithful and true to what she knew of God. I often wonder if God will show His mercy to her, because that's all she knew, and she was sure of His mercy. I miss her.

Losing someone you deeply love is never easy, but the hardest part of my grieving had been earlier, when I had last said goodbye to her in Somalia. My goodbye to her then had been meaningful, as I had known it would probably be the last.

In 1989 the news of my father's death reached me. This hit me harder. It was three in the morning when I received the call. I knew it was about my family. *I wonder how they know my number*, I asked myself. After a few rings I picked up: "*Allu, allu.*" On the other end was my best friend, who lived in Dubai at the time. I knew that she did not have good news—nothing good happens at three in the morning. After lighthearted conversation, inquiring how each other's families were doing, I asked her if all was well with my family. A pause. Then, "No, my sister," she replied.

"Who is it?" I asked.

"It's your father," she replied. "He died two days ago."

Long silence. "Are you there?" she inquired.

I think I said yes, because I heard her saying, "I am so sorry. May you be comforted by Allah. I will call you later." And she hung up.

The room spun as I lay on the floor in a fetal position, weeping from the depth of my soul like a weaned child. I did not have anyone to grieve with me. My family was thousands of miles away, so the grief and the loss were mine and mine alone. I wanted to wail for my dad, but three-in-the-morning wailing in this country was not conducive to the culture, so I whimpered instead.

Muslims bury their dead within a day of death, but intense mourning goes on for at least one week. During that time people wail and cry together, and they sit with the mourners in silence, with plenty of food and tea. Usually friends and distant relatives serve the mourners so that the mourning family does not have to do anything else. Wealth and inheritances are not discussed. A final feast ends the mourning period on the fortieth day after the death, after which it is time to let the dead go and move on. It signifies a new beginning. People are refreshed through washing rituals. The widow finishes her purification period. She is washed and takes off her mourning clothes, and then she enters society as a widow. This feast provides closure.

But here I was all alone with my grief. No mourning period, no feast, no rituals, no wailing—just a whimper. Gathering neighbors and friends to mourn with me was not feasible. So here I was alone. Or was I? I prayed to Allah, the unknowable God, to help me do my daily routines of taking care of my kids and my work. Somehow the help came, and what I needed for that day was given to me. I managed to live under the sun.

I did not pursue God in any way, because I had failed miserably trying different spiritual practices and had come up empty-handed.

* * * * *

It is strange that I had never heard anything about Christianity. Had God shielded me from Christians so that I could try everything else and come up empty-handed? Or is this an indictment of the Christians who would not share the greatest gift of all?

I thought of going back to Islam, but the endless rituals were hard to take—purifying oneself through methodical washing five times a day and being concerned about having been in contact with a male. Muslims have to repeat the washing ritual if they touch a dog or an unclean animal or if they see or touch a dead person. On and on it goes. But gossip, malice, lying, hatred, unforgiveness, judgmental attitudes—they have no way to avoid these issues of the heart. Muslims know that it is wrong to do or think these things, but Islam provides no power to help people resist them. This is the dilemma that Muslims and those of every other religion struggle with. Knowing to do right but instead doing wrong is the horizontal life of humanity without God.

I continued to spiral spiritually. My life was flatlined and horizontal, but my two beautiful and bright kids whom I adored and who depended on me kept me going. They gave me strength to carry on, to stay busy, to keep up with the masses who filled my life with endless activity and noise.

Things I'd had difficulty with when I first came to the U.S. now became part of my daily routine. The culture encouraged me to be feminist, telling me that I was equal with men and could do anything that a man could do.

For a while I had trouble making sense of it. I felt unprotected and unsafe, but I was responsible for protecting myself and my kids. I had never experienced this before, for someone else always watched over me. Here I was in the spirit of feminism—I was in charge of myself.

By now I had become a U.S. citizen, and I inquired about getting my license to work as a nurse. My nursing license was good in the Middle East, but I found out that here I had to be licensed by the California State Board. I began studying for the exam, and in the meantime I found a job at a hospital as a nurse's assistant so that I could take care of my kids.

I liked my work, but to fend for myself was to lose my identity as a woman. As a feminist, I could not maintain my womanhood, because I was required to be someone I was not created to be. I was uncomfortable. But if I expressed my inadequacy, I would be seen as weak in a culture that promoted strength, self-esteem, and confidence.

It seemed to people that I must have issues from my childhood that drained my self-esteem. But that wasn't so. My trouble was that I thought I was better than a man. I really did not have any interest in competing with men. I knew that God had made me a female, and that was good enough for me. I knew in the depth of my soul that God was good, and everything He had made was good. To be a feminist actually diminished me. But being in a culture in which feminist thoughts were embraced compelled me to comply. So I learned not to expose my weakness or tenderness. To my mask of individualism was added the mask of feminism.

The lines were blurred—men trying to be women and women trying to be men. After all, we lived in a free society in which lines could easily be crossed.

I registered to vote. Now I was a liberal feminist *and* a Democrat. More confusion. I learned how to be shallow and not to share my deep thoughts. It was a superficial life with no meaning to speak of and no depth. My horizontal life continued.

And then utter despair.

* * * * *

A month after my father's death, another call came at three in the morning. My heart sank, and I let it ring for a while, hoping it would go away. I finally picked it up. "*Allu*," I said. My friend was on the other end again, and it occurred to me that I might have second thoughts about our friendship if she continued to bring bad news. Small talk again about life and kids, and finally the question came, "Is all well with my family?"

A long pause and then, "No, I am sorry!"

"Who is it this time?" I asked.

"Your brother Mohammed."

This time the phone dropped from my hand, and I collapsed. I could hear my friend yelling on the other end, "Maryama, Maryama, *allu*?" I could not pick up the phone; it was as if the life had drained from me. I kept saying, "My brother, my brother, you cannot be gone. It's not true, my brother, my brother."

My younger brother, Mohammed, had been killed by a classmate in school. This young man had methodically slit my brother's throat and left his body on the ground for days. My brother was not buried—there was no time or place to bury him, for the land was filled with blood.

In 1989 civil unrest began in my country, which led to a civil war. Besides my brother, the fighting destroyed and killed every man in my family who was of age except for one uncle who lived in Kenya. It also took from us our land, our livestock, our homes—everything was lost forever. The women with their young ones fled to the wilderness and hid. I heard that it was friend against friend, brother against brother, neighbor against neighbor. No one was spared; nothing was sacred. It was a country in flames.

My mind could not comprehend what was happening. I did not know who was alive or dead. In our small country people knew each other and broke bread together most of the time.

I had grown up in a land of peace, where we girls went to the cinema and walked home at eleven or twelve at night talking and laughing. The thought of someone harming us was unthinkable. Now I tried to absorb what was happening. Where had people gone wrong? What had happened to their consciences? How did a person just cut someone's throat with a dagger, especially someone that person knew and broke bread with? I came to realize that the country I had been raised in and had affinity with no longer existed.

Another loss, another grief, another mourning. But this time a burden of guilt overwhelmed me as well, since I had not been able to help my brother financially because I had been too focused on the affairs of my life.

I felt that his death was my fault, and that was a weight I could not carry. Not only had I lost him, but I was responsible for his death. Who would free me from this burden? The death of my brother along with the other deaths in my family took a toll on me, and I went into a period of despair.

But even in my darkness, I always seemed to sense a glimmer of hope. Hope was the anchor of life that helped me to go on, and I was thankful for that.

* * * * *

But I had no time to mourn. I had to search for the women and children hiding in the wilderness. How would I start?

At three in the morning, the phone rang once again. Why did it always have to be at three in the morning? I began to despise the nights; I still jump today when the phone rings after midnight. This time it was my younger half sister, Samia, who had been born to my father's new wife after my mother died. Samia and I wept bitterly together, and she brought me up to speed on all that had happened. She and my nephew were in Nairobi, and the rest of the family was in the wilderness. I comforted her, but who would comfort me?

We ended our conversation, me assuring her that they would be okay. Then I crawled back into bed and waited for the sun to come out. Somehow daylight makes things tolerable.

I did not have a plan; I did not know how to save them. All I knew was that they had to live, and I was the only hope they had. I could not look at my loss, my grief, the desolation; it was as if my mind shut down and would not allow me to be aware of anything except the task that was ahead of me. As I thought of how to navigate the journey ahead of me, the hope I always felt surged again, but this time it was stronger than before. I sensed something like a thick curtain and felt that if I could pull back that curtain, something awesome would be there. Strength came from that hope.

I had only three thousand dollars in my savings account, yet twenty-three women and underage kids waited for me to rescue them. Over the years I had put 6 percent of my income plus a little college money for Eda and Eric in a money market account. What I had not known is that the market had been booming, and I now found that the little I had saved had produced a great yield. I suddenly realized that I had enough money to rescue my family.

But the thought of using my kids' savings created a dilemma for me. Should I use the money to help my family, or should I save it for my kids? It was clear that saving lives was the decision I had to make. It was not an easy one, but in the end I knew that we lived in a country that values achievers, and that is what my kids were.

So I took the plunge. I wired money to my sister in Nairobi. My nephew had been studying in Egypt and had been on vacation in Nairobi when the war broke out, and he had no way of getting back to school, where he was about to graduate. So I sent money for him to go back and graduate, and I instructed my sister to return to Somalia, gather the family, and take them to Ethiopia, where travel was safer than in Kenya.

Within ten days my family was in Ethiopia. The amazing thing is that none of the women or children had been hurt or misused at any time that they'd been in the wilderness. It was as if some invisible hand had been watching over them.

Many people were abused and misused during the war, but not my family. The God who was in the shadows had protected them.

When my family arrived in Ethiopia, I told them to mourn for their dead and then to rest, eat, drink, and refresh themselves. They had never had a chance to mourn, which in our culture is so important to the healing process.

By this time refugees were being accepted throughout the Western nations, including the U.S. Even better, anyone who was related to a U.S. citizen was given priority for acceptance in the U.S.

The long procedure of processing twenty-three people and proving their legitimacy was overwhelmingly grueling. Most of the children had been born while I was in the U.S., so I studied their pictures, learned their ages and names, and memorized how each one was related to me in order to avoid any corruption. It was common for people to claim and sell names to others who were not related to them, but I did not do that. I did everything legitimately by the book; everything was done without a lie. And God had mercy on our family.

* * * * *

During the months following my father's and brother's deaths, as I worked to secure my family's safety, Eda was coming of age—she was about twelve—and conflict was emerging in our relationship. All my confusion, pain, and loss had spilled over into my relationship with my daughter—not to mention that the money that had been for her schooling was now being used to save lives. She had every right to be angry with me, but I knew that we would weather the storm. She had a good foundation and was very bright, and I was confident that she would take her place in the world.

I had taught her early in life that instead of becoming a secretary, she should *have* a secretary, and instead of being a cheerleader, she should be the player. Her values and self-image did not come from Hollywood or the glitters of television but from within—from a core foundation of knowing that she was valued. The conflict of having a third-world mother who viewed the world, family, culture, and community through lenses other than that of American individualism threatened to separate her from me, and my efforts to hang on to her created a great strain between us. But she always remained my beloved daughter, and I knew that this strain in our relationship would not last forever.

Eric, my son, was coming along fine. He was less challenging than Eda, maybe because he was much younger, only about six at this time, and he had the privilege of being the second child with a more experienced and more tolerant mom.

During this time I became indifferent and cynical. I did not know how to navigate or process the pain, loss, and grief I was experiencing. I carried such a burden on my shoulders—twenty-three people depending on me and so many details needing to be seen to. I was afraid that if I opened my feelings and wounds, I would collapse and be unable to do anything, so I stuffed them down and put on a new mask.

I was not sure who I was with so many masks—one for every occasion. I looked good on the outside; my life appeared cohesive. But it was unraveling at the edges fast.

The process of bringing my family to the U.S. was arduous and the road too long.

My family found great comfort in Ethiopia. I cared for them, and they were safe and rested. We talked a lot and cried a lot. The U.S. government accepted my entire family, and they were instructed to travel to Kenya to be interviewed and to have their papers processed. Another journey. I gave them instructions and the means to go to Kenya. I felt relieved that the first part of this long ordeal was coming to a head. They still faced coming into a new culture and learning new ways of life here in America, but I was thankful at least that the hard part of getting them here was about to end.

5

THE CROSS IN VIEW

Jesus, the author and finisher of our faith . . . for the joy that was set before Him endured the cross, despising the shame, and has sat down at the right hand of the throne of God.
Hebrews 12:2

At the grocery store one day, I noticed a guy staring at me and following me around. When I finished shopping, he introduced himself and asked where I was from, because he had heard my accent (the story of my life—what is it with Americans and accents?). This man gave me his phone number and told me, "I would love to take you to dinner." I did not call him for a few days, playing hard to get, I suppose. When I finally called him, he made a dinner reservation for us at the Queen Mary, and we had a beautiful time.

We began dating, and before long he moved in with us. He became a great comfort in my life. He begged me to marry him and promised me a house with a white picket fence. I did not know what that meant, but later I found out that this was what American girls wanted. He could have offered me sheep and goats with a few camels in the country and won me. But I declined his offer. I wanted him in my life, but when it came to the idea of marriage, I just did not have anything to give.

My life continued with one tribulation after another. My relationship with my daughter got worse, and life became difficult and tiresome. What kept me going was the sense that something was within my grasp, but what was it? Or *who* was it?

Over the next few years my confusion over lost lives, lost country, lost culture passed. My family was safe and provided for. Now my self-awareness and the questions I'd had all my life were resurrected. My emptiness and the fear of death surged again.

* * * * *

In my early years in the U.S., I had met a girl whose parents were missionaries in Kenya. She had never really told me what their mission was, for I never asked. Years later I met another Christian girl who told me that Jesus had been killed by the Jews. Her words confirmed in my heart that Jewish people were troublemakers and had killed an innocent man. To me Jesus was just a good man; my friend never told me who Jesus was or why He had been killed, and again, I never asked. Despite all my searching for satisfaction in different religious practices, it never occurred to me to investigate Christianity, and nobody took the time to introduce it to me. I guess it was not my time.

But in July of 1994, God, who had been in the shadows all my life, broke through.

One day as I dropped my daughter off at summer school, I felt numb. The grief I had been acquainted with from my childhood through the fall of my country due to civil war came crashing in on me. For the first time I wailed violently. As I drove, I turned the radio up loud and started to wail so profoundly that I felt physically ill in a deep place where I had never felt pain before.

I pulled the car over and literally doubled up, my tummy heaving, and all I could utter was, "Allah God." I do not know how long I sat there, but when I opened my cloudy eyes, I saw a cross in front of me.

The cross stood on the top of a church, and as I focused on it, my sight became clearer. For the first time in all the years I had been in the U.S., I was looking at a cross. Had I seen one before? I am sure I had! But I had never looked at one intently the way I did this time. I was convinced that there was a story in that cross and that the story had something to do with me—but what?

I drove into the parking lot of the church. I sat in the car for a while, still fixated on this cross, contemplating whether I should go in and what I would say.

I got out of my car, my eyes bloodshot from crying, and entered the building. It was a quiet little church, and a properly dressed woman greeted me and asked if she could help me. Sheepishly I answered, "Of course! Could you tell me about the cross?"

"I beg your pardon?" she answered.

"I saw the cross on your building, and I want to know more about it!" I stated. The woman obviously noticed that I was in distress, but she was perplexed at the idea of someone inquiring about the cross in this day and age in the heart of Orange County, where there is a cross at almost every corner.

She invited me to sit down and went back to the office. In a little while a gentleman appeared, very pleasant but perplexed as well. "Can I help you?" was his question.

"Yes, please! Can you tell me about the cross? I saw the cross on your building, and I am interested to know more about it."

"What do you want to know about it?" was his reply.

"I am a Muslim. Well, actually, I do not know what I am, but I am in deep distress from many things that have happened in my life, including the destruction of my country due to civil war and the loss of my family. Everything I knew and valued in life is gone, and I am looking for meaning in all this." I explained how I had seen the cross, which I had never noticed before, and that I wanted to know the meaning of the cross. The man asked my name, phone number, and address, and strangely enough I gave them to him—or was I compelled to do so?

They asked me if I would agree to them coming to my house once a week for four weeks and also if I would attend church every Sunday during those weeks. The home visits would be to show a film each week about the Bible from beginning to end. I agreed, and the pastor of the church promised to call me. I went home expectantly.

My boyfriend was a good man who cared much for us. His family also loved us, especially his mom. That evening when he came home, he told me that he was struggling with drugs and wanted to stop. He told me that he had gone to a church and invited the elders to come to share with us about God, and would I mind if they came on Wednesday?

I'd had no clue that he was struggling with drugs. He had never used at home and never introduced me to them. I am thankful that my boyfriend (or Someone else?) protected me from drugs, because I found out later that his friends and their wives all struggled with them. These people appeared to be doing well in life and never had the image of users, but they were addicts.

While we were talking, the phone rang, and it was this elder saying that he and others from his church would come on Wednesday to explain the cross. It happened to be the same church that my boyfriend had asked to help him and his godless girlfriend! So we agreed to the plan. My boyfriend wanted to quit drugs, and I wanted to know the God who knew me.

* * * * *

On Wednesday evening we ate dinner early, and the kids did their homework. By seven thirty we were ready to hear what they had for us. Many thoughts were going through my head, the most recent being about my boyfriend and his issues with drugs—as if I did not have enough trouble with my own issues. But this time I did not have the energy to process or to fight anything. I was more focused on what I would hear when these men visited us. I was hopeful. Was it another Scientology or like all the other religious practices I had tried, or was there something deeper? The cross was seared in my mind. What was the connection between my aching soul and the cross? My anticipation grew, and the awaited appointment finally came.

The gentlemen came with a video tape, and we all sat down and watched what I thought would be a movie, but it was the story of God and His creation. It captivated me. There was something about it that resonated with me unlike any other religious or spiritual experience I'd had. I focused intently on everything I heard, and before I knew it, it was over. The hour had gone like a blink, and I had to wait another week.

But the elders had invited us to church on Sunday, so we went.

We took communion at the church—I did not know what it meant. My son, now nine, asked if he could have more grape juice, and when I asked the usher if he could have more, I was totally denied. The usher was disgusted with my request and said no! My son asked me why he could not have more grape juice, and I told him I did not know—maybe the church was having a shortage of grape juice. I do not remember hearing a clear explanation of the communion; I was processing so much information that I must have missed it.

That day I took my first communion without truly understanding its ramifications. I felt a little different as I tried to digest all that I had heard on Wednesday and was now hearing in the Sunday sermon. I was still processing the creation story, and in the sermon Jesus was discussed. I could not make the connection between the two teachings, but something about the name of Jesus comforted me. I was still mesmerized with the cross I had seen. God gave me a measure of patience to see this through, and I had a glimmer of hope and anticipation.

During the four weeks that we were visited by the elders, I saw many parallels between what I was hearing and what I had heard before in Islam, but with discrepancies. In Islam Abel killed Cain, and Abraham sacrificed Ishmael instead of Isaac. In Islam I had heard about Noah, Abraham, Lot, Joseph, Moses, David, Solomon, Essa (Jesus), and Mohammed. They were all prophets sent by Allah to show people the way of God, and Mohammed was his last and favorite prophet. Essa, or Jesus, had been born to a virgin, Maryam, but to call Him the Son of God was a blasphemy worthy of death.

Seeing these videos was a God thing, because it gave me a full spectrum of the story of salvation. I was mesmerized and overwhelmed at times because of the discrepancies I saw between Islam and Christianity, but the whole story was so gripping that I had to watch it to the end.

Then I saw the story of Jesus—who He was and what He did. I loved the story! Jesus knew who He was, and He spoke with certainty and authority. He was kind and gentle. I saw that He was a shepherd, and thus I realized His love for me, because I knew the heart of a shepherd. For a shepherd to die for his sheep was comprehensible to me. Everything changed—I fell in love immediately. There was something beautiful about Him; I felt that He knew me. It seemed to me that everything I had ever wanted was in Him.

I was crushed that He had gone to the cross, for I did not grasp the magnitude of His death and the reason why He had died. I did not yet understand that Jesus was God. But I was willing to follow Him as a prophet, for He was very nice, and I felt good about Him. Considering the condition of my soul, this was wonderful news.

But there was more. I heard that Jesus went to the cross not on His behalf but on my behalf and that if I believed in Him, my sins would be forgiven and I would be in paradise when I died. I made the connection between the cross and Jesus.

This was too much good news. I could not believe my good fortune. That Sunday at church I asked, "What must I do?"

"Believe in the Lord Jesus, and you will be saved."

"What else?" I asked.

"Nothing else," was the reply.

I got up with my two kids, one on each side of me, and we went forward and prayed. Immediately we were taken to be baptized, and we were given a certificate of our new birth. I did not know much, and I had no expectation that things would change for me here on earth, but I had the assurance that I would go to heaven when I died, and that was good enough for me.

I did not think that God had good things for me here and now. I only knew that I was forgiven and heaven bound—I would not have to face the judgment to come that my grandmother used to talk about. I was amazed and blessed to have this awesome fellowship and the privilege of knowing Him, which was never ending. I had been blind, but now I could see.

I could not comprehend it, but I accepted the gift graciously. I was okay to fend for myself in life. I was totally thankful and content simply to know that I was forgiven.

* * * * *

That day after church I felt tired, as if a weight I had been carrying all my life had just been lifted off. I fell asleep in the afternoon and had sweet rest.

That evening we went to church for a potluck. It was my first fellowship as a believer with God's people and my Savior. I did not bring anything and was embarrassed, but the small congregation was kind and gracious. There was plenty of food.

But it was strange food—pork, sausage, and other kinds of food that Muslims did not eat. All of a sudden I stood back and thought, *What took place today? I am a Christian, and this will be my diet.*

A lady behind me said, "Come, dear, grab a plate and dig in."

"I am a Muslim," I told her. "I do not eat this food."

"You are not a Muslim; you are a Christian now."

For a moment I was vexed in my spirit. But at that moment wisdom came to me, and I said to myself, *Wouldn't I still be a Christian if I did not eat the food that is from pigs?*

My beloved sweet Jesus whom I had just met that morning spoke through a godly woman named Pearl, and she told me that I did not have to eat pork.

This was the beginning of God speaking to me countless times a day, whether through His people, the Scriptures, prayer, or meditation. My blissful journey of knowing God had begun.

PART 2

THE LIGHT OF THE CROSS

6

SEEKING GOD, FINDING JESUS

O Death, where is your sting?
O Hades, where is your victory?
1 Corinthians 15:55

I did not know much about Jesus at first. I just knew that if I put my trust in Him, I would go to heaven. And at some point early in my faith I came to understand that He was the Son of God. That's all I knew.

I experienced a peace I'd never had before. The fact that I would not be judged by God after I died was too wonderful to believe. And I noticed something else: I was no longer against the Jewish people. As a matter of fact, I had an affection toward them. Now this was strange to me, because I had been taught that the Jews were the enemies of God,

Allah, and that no Muslim should have any dealings with them. So feeling affection toward them was something I had never dreamed of. I knew that something of great magnitude had happened in my life. Peace, no fear of death, and loving Jews—I pondered these things.

I had never owned or read a Bible, but now I acquired my first one, and I started reading from the beginning. But this did not go too well for me. Some discouragement set in, and I was overwhelmed. But I had a great desire to know Jesus.

One morning I had an urgent need to pray, and I did not know how. You see, in Islam we wash and clean in certain methodical ways, and because God was now so holy and precious to me, and I was so thankful for what He had done for me, I did not want to blow it. As I looked through the Bible, my eyes fell on Psalm 42:1–2: "As the deer pants for the water brooks, so pants my soul for You, O God. My soul thirsts for God, for the living God. When shall I come and appear before God?"

Joy filled my heart, and I felt the weight of His glory. He had visited me and revealed Himself to me in a way that only a shepherdess would comprehend, for I remembered well seeing a deer panting for water. When it came to the brook, it dipped its feet in the water and drank almost a minute or two; then it took a moment to breathe and linger before drinking more. Then slowly and gracefully it walked away, satisfied. My soul was thirsty for the living God. My Lord showed me my great need for Him, and He put in my heart a thirst that no one could quench except Him.

I became undone and found myself facedown. You see, I had always thought that in order to worship God, I had to go through cleansing rituals, which are tiresome and tedious, but I saw that this God was different. He was not burdensome.

The book of Psalms was instrumental for me as I began getting to know Him, because it was a book of poetry about God reaching out to man and man responding to God. It was about a human soul seeking a safe harbor, and it was full of pain, sorrow, joy, praise, worship, and thanksgiving. It was a beautiful dialogue between humanity and their Creator, who yearned for them. The book of Psalms was about a God of holiness, love, mercy, and grace, a just God who was true to Himself and could not deny Himself. Psalm 119 got me every time.

The other book I read was the Gospel of John. In John I saw that Jesus was the Shepherd and that I, the little Somali shepherdess, was a sheep. There I first understood the extent of His love. Just as a good shepherd cares for his sheep, so Jesus was watching over me, guiding me to green pastures, taking me to still waters. He satisfied my soul.

As I read, I learned to hear His voice and follow Him. He was the Good Shepherd, and I was becoming a sheep, even though at times I tended to be a goat. Goats are unruly and stubborn; they stray from the flock and can be vicious. But my Jesus began taming this goat to be a sheep.

* * * * *

I became a member of the small congregation that had taught me about Jesus. It was mostly an older crowd, which was good for us; my children and I were loved and nurtured. But there was no in-depth Bible study; the teaching was mainly topical, about parenting or giving or some other issue. A few hymns were sung each service, and that was it for the week. But I learned the Word through reading it.

And I had a lot to learn. On the day of my spiritual birth, six people had been saved and baptized. Three days later the pastor had transitioned to heaven. His departure was hard on me, because I thought my sin was so great that it had caused the pastor who had baptized me to die.

As I mentioned before, my boyfriend and I were introduced to the Lord at the same time, and he too was saved. But as it turned out, we received Jesus for different reasons. He wanted something from Jesus, and I wanted Jesus. Needless to say, as I began to cultivate this new relationship with Jesus, one day my boyfriend realized that these new changes were not for him. He felt that I was taking my newfound faith too far, and he didn't like how it was affecting our relationship.

For the first time in my life, I was dumped. So tough on the ego—but it was the beginning of my process of being reduced. In a way I was relieved, because it was too hard to love two guys at the same time. Jesus was moving too fast for my boyfriend—He was invading my life. So Jesus won, and He changed the locks on my life and posted a sign out front: NEW MANAGER AND OWNER.

The amazing thing is that my boyfriend and I did not fight. There was no anger. He truly did care for me and my kids, and I truly cared for him. He actually bought my daughter a car when she turned sixteen, and when he moved out, he gave us twenty-five thousand dollars to carry us through. Was that Jesus or what? I did not know much about trust, but I loved Him.

I kept reading my Bible, seeking more of Jesus. I lingered in the book of Psalms and in the Gospel of John for a while, because I loved what I was reading. I believe that is what Jesus wanted me to learn for a while.

One day while I was in the car, I stumbled on this odd-sounding voice, and I remembered hearing it almost fourteen years ago. The voice had frightened me then because it had been speaking about an unknown religion, so I had changed the station immediately and had never heard it since. Now it was not repulsive. It was gentle, clear, and soothing to my ears. It was the voice of Dr. J. Vernon McGee. He had started a five-year study through the Bible, and he was just laying the foundation and was about to start the book of Genesis.

I was ecstatic. There was no doubt in my mind that this was the doing of the Lord, my Savior, who had drawn me out of darkness and into the light. I thank Him often for that famous day that He put me on a path of learning, studying, and meditating on the Word of God precept by precept. I was on cloud nine and in love. That encounter put me on a solid rock of getting to know the sweetest Person I have known and will ever know.

The Word of God truly became bread of life for my body and spring water for my soul. The world became beautiful, the colors more vibrant. I felt balanced. Before I had always felt lopsided. I had lived in a world of shadows with no reality; now things became real to me. My mind was sound for the first time in my life. I had clarity of thought, and I found meaning, purpose, and direction.

I began experiencing God's presence every morning. Each day was now new and fresh, full of expectation. My steps were lighter. No more fear of death—I had the promise of heaven. This was life.

As I grew in the faith through studying the Word with Dr. McGee, I learned that I could call God a Father. It was strange at first for me to call God, who is holy, a Father! But as He drew me in, I began to be comfortable with the concept, and each day as I learned to listen to and talk with Him, my love for Him grew, and His love for me was revealed to my heart.

Then one day, about a year and a half after I was saved, I heard on the radio that the Holy Spirit was God. I had never heard of God the Holy Spirit, and I was shocked. I thought to myself, *There is another God?* By now I had come to understand that Jesus was God, and of course I knew that the Father was God. A fear of being deceived entered my mind, and I began to spin. The idea of worshiping many gods frightened me. My mind went back to Islam, which says that there is one God, and now I had three.

I almost slipped. But since I was learning that God was my Father, I thought I should ask Him, and this is what I said: "Abba"—that is how we say "father" in the Somali language—"Abba, I need Your help. I don't want to worship multiple gods, because I believe that You are one, but I am hearing about Jesus, God, and now the Holy Spirit. How can this be?"

A few minutes later on the radio I heard about a church that was about to teach on God the Holy Spirit for four weeks. Prayer answered! I was ready to learn about the Holy Spirit.

* * * * *

This new church was filled with people of different groups, colors, and ages. There was a full band—it was like being at a concert except that people were of a sound mind, raising their hands and worshiping God. I thought that I had died and gone to heaven.

The Holy Spirit was explained. Although I did not have a full grasp of Him, I understood that He had a full grasp of me: He is the One who had put the desire to know God in me. He is the One who now prompted me to read the Bible and to pray. He gave me wisdom. He revealed and illuminated to me God the Father and God the Son. He was my comforter, my counselor, and my director, and He was involved in my daily life in ways that I could not even comprehend.

I grew rapidly in this church. I went to church as many times as possible in a week. I could not stop talking about Jesus—He was indeed the lover of my soul. I was a new creation. Everything in my life was being renewed.

But there were struggles too. Even though my old self had been put to death positionally in God's economy, practically it was still alive and causing havoc in my life. It seemed as if I had become two people, the old self and the new self, and they were at war with each other.

The old self never had any competition—she came and went as she pleased. It was all about her. She had many masks and packages, and if she was capable of doing any good, it was to her advantage. She was all about self-preservation. She wanted to be loved, accepted, respected, adored, or even flattered. It was all about self.

Then a new person had emerged out of the ashes, and she wanted to do good, to love mercy, and to walk humbly before her God.

How could I reconcile these two? I found that it was not possible—one had to die. Jesus said that the old self had to be put to death, and it would be a lifelong journey, one day at a time.

My life as a Christian was blossoming. Even though there was not much of significance to see on the outside, I knew that I was changing from within.

Meanwhile, my Somali family was about to arrive in the U.S. I was overjoyed that my family—what was left of it—was about to unite with me, and I could not wait to share my good news of Jesus with them. I told them that I had a secret to share when they arrived. Some of them were scared to hear that, but I assured them that I had good and awesome news.

7

STRENGTHENED TO STAND IN THE NEW LIFE

Watch, stand fast in the faith, be brave, be strong.
1 Corinthians 16:13

My relationship with the Lord continued to deepen. I had learned to anticipate what God had for me each day, and I had also become confident that God was for me and loved me. Now I was anxious to learn how to pray and worship.

And I needed to learn, because the Lord knew that I needed to be strongly anchored in my faith before my family came.

Some Christians encouraged me to ask God for stuff in prayer, but I felt funny doing that. I was more interested in knowing Him, the Giver, instead of having gifts. The mere fact that I was forgiven was more than my heart could handle.

To me He was enough, and His forgiveness was more than enough, and I had no desire for material stuff or blessing on this earth. We had a safe place to live, we ate well, we were healthy, and we were heaven bound—what more could we ask for? Giving thanks to Him was in order.

But I was about to learn that not only was I heaven bound, but God did want to bless me with all spiritual blessings and materially as well so that I could be a blessing to others. Heaven will be great, but I came to see that earth is the game changer. I was created to glorify Jesus in my life here and now, to be a light that shuns darkness, to illuminate and reveal His beauty and goodness, to share His pain in a world that has rejected Him, to speak for Him and to defend and honor His name, to be His child, friend, and inheritance. "For the eyes of the LORD run to and fro throughout the whole earth, to show Himself strong on behalf of those whose heart is loyal to Him" (2 Chronicles 16:9).

Being loyal to Him and not having a divided heart was His requirement of me, and He even promised me to empower me to do so. Glorious.

I attended a seminar of prayer and worship, and it radically changed my life. I learned to worship God and to spend time with Him in the morning, and that became valuable as I grew in knowing God and walking with Him. My prayer time became alive.

I began each day with praise and worship. "Good morning, Father God, Lord Jesus, and Holy Spirit," I said. "Thank You for this glorious morning and for the start of a new day with You and all its promises. Lord Jesus, open the eyes of my heart that I may see the wondrous works of Your Word and the glorious splendor of Your majesty. Holy, holy, holy is the Lord God Almighty, who was and is and is to come." I continued talking about who God is, interweaving His attributes with praise and thanksgiving. I ended with Exodus 15:11: "Who is like You, O Lord, among the gods? Who is like You, glorious in holiness, fearful in praises, doing wonders?"

Then I proceeded to confession, standing on the finished work of God: "If we confess our sins, He is faithful and just to forgive us our sins and to cleanse us from all unrighteousness" (1 John 1:9). I knew that my sins had already been forgiven on the cross by the blood of Jesus and that positionally I was in good standing with God, but I was asking God to open the chambers of my heart and see if there was anything there that was not of Him. I simply allowed Him to clean His dwelling place so that our fellowship was not hindered. Selah! (I learned that "Selah" is a word in the Psalms that means to stop and consider.) I then paused to hear from Him, for He said, "Be still, and know that I am God" (Psalm 46:10). I waited to see if anything surfaced, and by His Spirit I gently released anything He showed me and gave Him permission to work in my heart.

Then I moved to intercession and prayer. I prayed for my Somali family and for my newfound family, the church of Christ, and I also lifted up those individuals whom the Lord put on my heart each day.

Now I was ready to face the world, because I had been with Jesus.

As I grew in His grace, I learned that my precious Lord was interested in every aspect of my life: my relationship with Him and others, my work, my health, my finances, my thoughts, my feelings, my heart. In short, He was invading my life, and I could not resist, because I found no fault in all He wanted to do. His pure and unadulterated love was irresistible.

* * * * *

My family arrived safely in the United States with no problems. I was elated to see them. I wept much for joy and mourned for the dead ones.

A lot of work now needed to be done. For the first two weeks after their arrival, from morning to evening, I took them to immigration, to the health clinic, to the schools, to the Social Security office. They were two weeks of utter exhaustion, but the Lord strengthened me.

My family was eager to hear the great news that I wanted to share with them, but I wanted them to rest first and to allow myself time to take care of the needs at hand. I reassured them that I would share with them after all the tasks were done.

Finally the day came when I was to share with them my great news. I told them, "I found God, and His name is Jesus." It seemed that the life drained from their faces as with total amazement they stared at me without a word.

After what seemed an eternity, they started to weep, but their weeping was for me. You see, their thought had been that at last Allah had brought them to this strange country to further their Islamic religion, and they would start with their lost sister. It came to my understanding that they had no intention of hearing about Christianity and that in their hearts I was dead to them. Not only would they have nothing to do with Jesus, but I was disowned and cut off.

I immediately realized that I was alone, and fear set in. But wait—I was not alone. All those months when I had been learning to pray and worship and get into the Word, God had been preparing me and anchoring me so that I could fall back on Him.

That night I went to bed bruised, but Satan was crushed, because my Jesus helped me to stand and not deny Him.

For the first time the thought of being disowned by my people for the sake of Christ became real to me. But what was clearer to me was the realization that I had seen and tasted the goodness of the Lord. I actually felt the door shut behind me, and there was no going back. The only way I could go was forward with Jesus.

The next morning when I woke up, I said as always, "Good morning, Father God, Lord Jesus, Holy Spirit. I want to spend time with You in worship, but I am afraid bitterness has entered my heart toward my family, and it is a hindrance to our fellowship. I am having difficulty being with You because I am ashamed of what is in my heart, for You are holy." Selah.

As I sat quietly, I felt the weight of His glory, and the Lord took me back to the previous Sunday's teaching:

> [Jesus] went out from there and came to His
> own country, and His disciples followed him.

And when the Sabbath had come, He began to teach in the synagogue. And many hearing Him were astonished, saying, "Where did this Man get these things? And what wisdom is this which is given to Him, that such mighty works are performed by His hands! Is this not the carpenter, the Son of Mary, and brother of James, Joses, Judas, and Simon? Are not His sisters here with us?" So they were offended at Him.

But Jesus said to them, "A prophet is not without honor except in his own country, among his own relatives, and in his own house." Now He could do no mighty work there, except that He laid His hands on a few sick people and healed them. And He marveled because of their unbelief. (Mark 6:1–6)

There was my answer. I was profoundly grateful for my Jesus' assurance that He had been there before. That day it became evident to me that there is nothing in my life that the Word of God has not spoken of.

That moment I forgave my family, and I was able to worship my Jesus with a thankful and pure heart. Glorious!

My life continued to blossom, but not without trials for sure.

Different relations came to reason with me that the path I had chosen was from Satan and that I should repent from this awful sin. I found myself in a dangerous place, fighting for my life to keep the gift I had received. And though I did not doubt my faith, I entered into argument with my relatives, which in hindsight was not profitable.

I became defensive and at times lost my temper. I was unable to get a word in, and things did not go well for me. But the Lord stood with me, and I did not waver in my faith. I was not strong enough to debate with them, for Muslims are known for their debating skills. And as the apostle Paul said, "The message of the cross is foolishness to those who are perishing, but to us who are being saved it is the power of God. For it is written: 'I will destroy the wisdom of the wise, and bring to nothing the understanding of the prudent'" (1 Corinthians 1:18–19).

I remember the day that I regretted bringing my family here and sacrificing all my daughter's and son's savings to do it. But then I realized that it was an amazing thing that I had not shared Jesus with them until they were settled and established in the country. All the wisdom of God! If I had shared with them and been rejected earlier, I truly believe that it would have affected all the hard work I did for them— perhaps I would have been bitter or it would have sabotaged my efforts to help them. But now they no longer needed me. The work was done. They had not had to be afraid of me not helping them—our Lord Jesus had protected me and them. Now it was my part to share, and it was their choice to either choose God or reject Him.

I must say, though, that I was crushed not only that they rejected the greatest gift of all—God Himself—but also that I found myself outside looking in. I was no longer part of my family or the Somali community. Word spread rapidly that I was a Christian and no longer identified with Islam.

* * * * *

Now that I was comfortable worshiping God in word and spirit through adoration, praise, thanksgiving, confession (so that our fellowship was not hindered), petition, and supplication, then came worshiping God in my finances.

In all my learning the Lord never asked me to do something that was not clearly spoken of in His Word. And usually it was spoken of not once but several times. I found tithing mentioned in the Bible in Genesis 14:18–20, Nehemiah 10:37, Malachi 3:10, Deuteronomy 26:12, and Matthew 23:23. But for me it was simple mathematics: my God had given me 100 percent. He told me I could keep 90 percent of all He had given me, and He asked me to give Him 10 percent, and when I did, He promised to bless me. I thought it was a great bargain. What a deal!

I learned later that 10 percent was just a start. As I prospered, I gave more, and oh, how I was blessed!

God is not a debtor to anyone. He owns everything, and the fact that He asks us to give Him what is already His is indeed for our benefit, because He desires to include us in sharing His blessings, His kingdom. In other words, we are co-owners of His kingdom. How awesome is that! To realize this blessing was a great awakening for me, and the more I gave, the more I received. I loved honoring the Lord in everything.

As I contemplated worshiping God in its many forms—through the Word and the Spirit, in my thoughts and my substance—I considered the fact that loving and honoring Him was vertical. It was looking up. But we have the responsibility and privilege of loving people too—which is horizontal.

In Mark 12:28 one of the scribes asked Jesus, "Which is the first commandment of all?" Jesus answered,

> The first of all the commandments is: "Hear, O Israel, the LORD our God, the LORD is one. And you shall love the LORD your God with all your heart, with all your soul, with all your mind, and with all your strength." This is the first commandment. And the second, like it, is this: "You shall love your neighbor as yourself." There is no other commandment greater than these. (Mark 12:29–31)

These commands are also stated earlier in the Bible, in Deuteronomy 6:4–6 and Leviticus 19:18.

As I thought about loving God and loving others, suddenly the cross came into view. Vertical—loving God. Horizontal—loving people. When we love God and not people, the cross disappears, and when we love people and not God, the cross disappears. So I had to look intently at the cross in order to see God and then to see people as He sees them. "For God so loved the world that He gave His only begotten Son, that whoever believes in Him should not perish but have everlasting life. For God did not send His Son into the world to condemn the world, but that the world through Him might be saved" (John 3:16–17).

Loving God seemed easy to me, but loving people would be more challenging. It was not easy to love when I felt rejected and hurt. But the two were intertwined, and I could not have one without the other.

8

BURDENED BY LEGALISM

This is the love of God, that we keep His commandments. And His
commandments are not burdensome.
1 John 5:3

I am forever grateful for my second church, for this
congregation introduced me to the work of the Holy Spirit
and taught me how to worship God, and I gained many
beautiful brothers and sisters there. Yet it was in this church
that I almost stumbled.

As I listened carefully to the Bible teachers I heard each
week, somehow I began to get the impression that I had to
do something to keep my salvation. They never directly said
that, and I may have understood things wrongly because I
was a new believer who didn't know much, but this is the
impression I had.

The church seemed to put a heavy emphasis on people's daily failures. In every communion either the pastor or an elder got up and prophesied about the sins people were committing, and he invited us to come to the front so that we could be prayed for and forgiven. I was committing every one of those sins, either by thought or action, and I was going forward every service. It got to the point where I would just go to the front before they announced my sins of the hour in order to save time.

I became caught up in the endless busyness of the Christian life. I was involved in evangelism, apologetics, us versus them, politics, and winning America for Jesus, and I was prejudiced against anyone who was not a Christian. I was becoming puffed up.

I dragged my kids to church and pointed out their sins to them just as the church pointed out my sins to me. I became a taskmaster to them instead of being a mother who represented Jesus to them. I loaded on them burdens that they could not bear. In short, I was on my way to being a legalistic Christian, which in my mind is the worst thing to be. Legalistic Christians are aware of their sins yet lack the power to overcome them, so they try to do more to make God love them more, if that makes sense.

The more involved in these things I became and the harder I tried to please God by doing them, the more unhappy I was. Working, taking care of my kids, and contributing financially and physically to too many causes made me feel tired and burdened. I could only handle so much. I felt like I was back in Islam—following rules in order to be accepted. I had become so busy doing stuff for the Lord that I forgot to enjoy Him.

* * * * *

All this had an effect on my daughter, Eda.

Eda was fifteen when I got saved, and I did not realize that becoming a Christian was one soul at a time. I did not know that I should have sat down with my daughter to explain what was happening to me, since I myself did not have a full grasp of it. All I knew was that for the first time in my life, I did not have to run or seek for something I was missing, and I assumed that my new faith was also my children's. So my daughter never truly got a hold of the beauty of Jesus.

In Eda's defense, her faith really never had a chance to take root and blossom. The church we were attending when I first came to faith was doing mostly topical sermons and not explaining the Word of God in depth. Then Eda was asked to teach the first graders, so she could not hear even the topical sermons, and I did not know to guide her differently.

Between her own growing pains and my struggles with war, grief, loss, and the rescue of twenty-three people while I learned to stand like a baby in my newfound faith, my relationship with my daughter was lost in the translation, and precious time was lost. I deeply regret it.

Now we were attending a guilt-inducing church that seemed to always emphasize our shortcomings and all that we were doing wrong instead of encouraging us to enjoy the finished work of Christ and His fellowship. All Eda could hear were the things that were wrong with her and all that was wrong in the world. Perhaps this is not what was really taught—I have a tendency to hear what I am doing wrong. But between this perception from the church and a third-world mother who was putting unbearable demands on her, naturally this is what Eda heard, and she missed the beauty of Jesus. She needed a God of grace, mercy, and kindness who had undying love for her, and she was not getting that from the church or from home.

Eric was nine when I got saved, and as I mentioned, I took the kids with me when I went forward that day, thinking that they would also be saved. Eric did stay with the faith as he grew, as he was younger and his heart was more tender, but the years after my salvation were hard for my precious Eda, and I was not sensitive to the changes she was going through.

* * * * *

I started to believe that loving God was more complicated than I had at first thought. Even more troubling was loving people, as I had discovered when my family rejected me. I found myself trying to practice religion, and I became trapped in trying to please God in my own strength.

Now that I knew God, the temptation to think that I was worthy of His love and could somehow earn it by following the dos and don'ts of religion crept into my life. I just could not grasp the depth of God's grace. So I overestimated myself. Pride.

But what was it about me that I thought God loved so much? It was time for me to explore who I was apart from God.

I went first to the book of Genesis. In chapters 1 and 2, I saw the perfection of beauty, the earth teeming with life. Every time God created a new thing, He said that it was good, and when He created man and woman, He said that it was *very* good. Then He gave Adam dominion over the earth. God was satisfied and rested from creating on the seventh day. So far so good.

But in chapter 3 things didn't go so well. There I saw the temptation and fall of man. The blaming game began—Adam blamed Eve, Eve blamed the devil. So God dealt with each one of them in Genesis 3:14–19. Adam and Eve were sent out of the garden—separated from God because of their sin. The colossal failure of humanity had begun.

But note verse 15: there God said to Satan, "I will put enmity between you and the woman, and between your seed and her Seed; He shall bruise your head, and you shall bruise His heel." God was promising that one day a Savior would come and correct the mess that Adam and Eve had made by listening to Satan. It took almost the whole Bible to see this prophecy fulfilled.

Before they left the garden, God covered them with animal skins. That was the first sacrifice of life for life.

I am not a theologian, but I recognized quite clearly that trying to please God without God was impossible. Throughout Genesis I saw pride, murder, prejudice, lying, cheating, drunkenness, incest, idolatry, sexual immorality, covetousness, and the like, because once Adam and Eve sinned and were separated from God, man became inherently bad. It is not that man *did* bad things—man *himself* was bad.

We are in reality contaminated seed, and contaminated seed begets contaminated seed.

I looked at the book of Romans, and it said the same thing. The apostle Paul distinctly states our utter helplessness to know God and please Him (see Romans 7:18–19). We are rotten seed through and through. If God hadn't acted by sending Jesus to die for us and restore us to God, we would have been doomed, separated forever from the source of goodness: God Himself.

I saw that all the heartache I had suffered before getting saved was the result of being separated from my Creator. And now here I was, as a Christian, trying to please Him on my own!

My endeavor to evaluate myself in the light of God came to nothing. On my own I was a sinner—nothing more. I found nothing to stand on and could only fall on the cross.

I saw a glimpse of God's broken heart over man's sin when He asked Adam in Genesis 3:9, "Where are you?" That question still echoes to each one of us: "Where are you?" Adam had failed, and all of us fail. Therefore, we needed another who could mediate between man and God—the man Jesus.

Thankfully, no matter how rotten we are, God's perfect goodness is just as profound. Throughout the Bible I saw His patience, mercy, loving-kindness, goodness, grace, and compassion—and His relentless pursuit of rebellious humanity. It is because of His goodness that we are not consumed and by His grace that we are rescued. Not one of us can earn or maintain salvation by doing all kinds of things for God.

I concluded that it was more profitable and fitting to know God than to know self. What I was without God frightened me. The intention to do well was with me, but I lacked the power to do it. But this is what Jesus offers—the power to do well and the heart to pursue God's goodness. This is where the road of losing self and gaining Jesus begins.

* * * * *

As I examined all that I had been doing for God and my efforts to love my family, I saw that ultimately my actions were borne of pride—a focus on what *I* could do for Him. And of all the sins that a man is capable of committing against God, pride is a stench in His nostrils. It promotes the illusion of self-sufficiency. It takes God's place in our lives, and it is offensive to Him. It ties God's hands to rescue us, and it is lifted up like an umbrella so that God's grace won't fall on us. The basis of humanity's fall is pride—we think that we can do a better job than God, that we are the captain of our destiny.

There is no remedy for pride except humility. God wanted me to have a broken heart and a contrite spirit so that He could lavish His grace and mercy upon me. I realized that every fiber of my being had to be brought under the subjection of Jesus Christ. Focusing on my faults and on my kids' faults was not helping any of us grow. I had to learn to surrender to Jesus daily—often many times in a day. My mind became a battlefield of good and evil; I had to choose, sometimes minute by minute, to meditate on God and remember who He is and what Jesus had done for me.

I had to learn how to be secure in the gift of salvation rather than in my efforts. The Bible clearly states that salvation is a gift from God and not of ourselves. I was saved simply because I had acknowledged and received with a grateful heart that Jesus had died in my place and risen again from the grave. I was completely forgiven of my past, present, and future offenses against God and would be with Him forever through eternity. He promised that He would always be with me and that I would never be alone. And *He* would give me the power to live a victorious life here on this earth. Life with Jesus. Glory!

I had gained Jesus, and I saw that now Jesus had to gain me. The only way I could overcome self was through the blood of Jesus Christ—life for life, just as I had seen in Genesis.

Both Genesis and Romans discredit human life without God. As I reconciled my heart with these two books (which actually echo the story of the whole Bible—a love story of God pursuing unlovable people and seeking to infuse His very life into us), my wretchedness was uncovered and the grace of God was revealed in me. As I came to God with empty hands, an open heart, and a receptive spirit, God told me, "I can work in you and through you."

Genesis and Romans helped me to eliminate any thought of bringing anything to God except my wretchedness and showed me that our very wretchedness is indeed a gift from Him. I do not know how this works, but it is one of the many mysteries of God.

* * * * *

God, as always, continued to be faithful, blessing me immeasurably, being patient and longsuffering in my schizophrenic Christian life. He who had done a good work in me would be faithful to complete it (see Philippians 1:6). All the while my Lord never left me—He was in me and for me.

I learned quickly not to *do* stuff but to *abide* in Him. Abiding meant living in Him, resting in Him, staying close to Him, and letting Him do the work. He was delighted to work in me, with me, and through me.

I revisited where I had started my faith: I had been saved by grace through faith in Christ Jesus (see Ephesians 2:8–9). Ephesians 1:13 showed me my ongoing position in Him: I had been sealed by the Holy Spirit, and therefore I was kept by Him. Galatians 3 also taught me to beware of adding to Christ—to beware of the peril of legalism. I began to see that since I had been saved by grace, I was also *kept* by grace. I was kept in my daily walk with Christ by abiding in Him and not by works.

As I set out on a quest to apply the Word of God in my everyday life, abiding in Christ began. The Word of God became precious to me and the name Jesus the love of my life. I came to love the hymn that says, "Jesus, Your name is like honey on my lips, Your Spirit like water to my soul. Your Word is a lamp unto my feet." These words spoke of my heart—Jesus' home.

Looking back, I realized that I had been learning too many things about God too fast. Some of what I heard was true of Him, but some of it was not, and my young spiritual life was unable to discern the difference. When I listened to

Bible teaching on the radio, I was filled with joy, but when I heard Bible teachers emphasize rules and dos and don'ts, it tripped me up, and I became discouraged and confused. My spiritual growth was in danger from gaining a lot of information with no depth.

Thankfully, I was extremely guarded in the early years of my spiritual growth. When I sensed that something was wrong, I went back to the Word of God. I had left so much behind—my country, my culture, my religion, my boyfriend, my family; having given up so much to follow Jesus, I did not want to be deceived. If being a Christian meant being legalistic and following a list of rules and rituals, I might as well have returned to Islam!

I almost lost the joy of being with Jesus, but He loved me too much to let that happen. He led me, taught me, guarded me. After all, He was my Shepherd.

9

THE KEY TO VICTORY: MY LIFE, JESUS' LIFE

To [the saints] God willed to make known what are the
riches of the glory of this mystery among the Gentiles:
which is Christ in you, the hope of glory.
Colossians 1:27

I worked as a nurse's assistant for several years, and during
that time I continued studying for my nursing exam. But I
meandered from my studies, partly because so many things
were happening in my life and partly because the role of
nursing was rapidly changing too. I noticed that nursing
contained less and less direct nurse-patient contact, at least
here in the U.S.

This troubled me. My reason for wanting to be a nurse
was that I wanted to love and take care of sick people; I

was not interested in policies and procedures and worrying about being sued.

But God had other ideas for me. I heard on the radio one day about a school of holistic massage, which interested me, as this kind of work ministered to patients in a comprehensive way. God providentially supplied the funds for me to attend the school, so I laid aside my nursing aspirations and left my job at the hospital, and I flourished in my new studies.

Afterward I found a job doing holistic massage for a hospice company, where my need to care for and nurture the sick was greatly satisfied. And my pay was comparable to that of a registered nurse! God is so good.

* * * * *

As I came out of a legalistic mind-set and began letting go of my pride and self-effort and busyness, I began to understand that I didn't belong to a religious organization but was a part of a living organism. I was part of the body of Christ, as the apostle Paul clearly states in 1 Corinthians 12:27.

Christ is the head of the body. Just as our natural body is controlled by our head, or our mind, so we as believers are controlled by Jesus, who is the mind of the body—the church of Christ. I had become a unit of an organism that had the mind of Christ. This meant that my mind and body were under subjection to Christ, and I needed to be saturated with Christ, mind, body, and spirit. The flesh, the world, and Satan had been dethroned.

The Lord was showing me that I needed to be a good steward of my senses. If Jesus had control of my mind—my intellect, thoughts, emotions, feelings—then He was truly my master. Only in this way could I know Him, His character, His desires, His plans for me and for the world. As He infused Himself into me, His heartbeat of love, compassion, mercy, and grace would become real to me.

My senses became extremely sensitive to the things going on around me in the culture. My senses and thought processes were fine-tuned, and things that had been okay for me to hear and see before were not easy for me to bear anymore.

I did not have to think about this and decide, "I am not going to do this thing anymore." I just began to find myself in awkward places, and that is when I realized that my senses belonged to Jesus. It was as if I was now looking at the world through His eyes, so I had to guard against what I exposed my eyes and ears to. As I learned to see the beauty of the Word of God and hear the joyful sound of the Lord, the world around me seemed contaminated somehow.

I had a difficult time grasping how to navigate this new life, however, in a broken world, with the old self trying to be revived. At times I said things or reacted in ways that offended people. When you are in love with someone, you talk about him. So since I was in love with the greatest Guy the world has ever known, I wanted to tell people that they too could have this great love. But it was somehow offensive to them. I was dismayed, but later I found out that the Word says that the gospel is offensive to the unbelieving world. So I managed to ruffle some feathers in the culture and in my own family.

During this time of learning, my spiritual senses were sharpened, and my physical senses were being intertwined with my spiritual senses. Everything that I said, saw, or heard went automatically through the filter of the Holy Spirit, and all of a sudden I had clarity. Oh, how thankful I was for God the Holy Spirit. I was enjoying this amazing helper.

* * * * *

So my eyes became His eyes. Soon the television shows that had been okay with me were no longer okay with Him. Then He desired for me to take a break from television for a while.

One day at my work, during a quiet afternoon in the office, I heard the girls giggling and laughing about something they were watching on the computer. One of the girls called to me, "Hey, Maryama, come here and look at this." I truly felt uneasy about going and looking. So I cautiously went, and I saw a picture of the back of a man with no clothes on. The girls were admiring him and how good he looked. I did not see his front part—praise God for His protection.

Within a second I was screaming. I actually felt that my eyes had fallen, and for a moment I could not see. I held my hands to my face, and all I could say was, "Oh, my eyes, my eyes." At that moment everybody in the office came running, including the bosses, scared and asking if I was okay. I kept saying, "My eyes, my eyes."

That day because of my reaction, the company system was blocked from any compromising pictures. Evil was shunned that day from the computer system of that company simply because my eyes were Jesus' eyes.

* * * * *

Another day I was at the nursing station doing some charting, and a male nurse came to the station, angry, and used my Lord's name in a vile way. I put my hands over my ears, just I had done with my eyes, and started to sob. Everyone stopped and looked at me, and the male nurse asked if I was okay. Facing him, I said, "I love Him."

"I'm sorry!" He replied with a puzzled face.

"You used God's name in vain," I said. "He is precious to me."

"I am so sorry, ma'am," was his reply.

I thanked him for his apology. I finished my charting, but I lingered awhile to pray for that young man and to bless the place. He did not know that I prayed for him. My ears, Jesus' ears.

* * * * *

Jesus gave me my tongue so that He could speak through me to bless, encourage, build, and heal. But I must say that my tongue is the most challenging for me to manage, especially when it comes to my family. My tongue is a work in progress as I learn to intentionally choose words that will build and bless people.

One day I was walking down a long, busy hallway in the hospital on my way to visit a client. Some of the people I passed were talking, some were quiet, but everybody was absorbed in their lot. As I walked, I took in what was going on around me, and along the way I noticed a "Wet Floor" sign. Behind it was a woman mopping the floor, her face looking down at the floor. People passed her in each direction, but nobody noticed her.

When I reached her, I said, *"Buenos días!"* She looked up with amazement, and her beautiful brown eyes lit up as if she had received a precious gift. Her countenance softened with a lovely smile that showed her front gold tooth, and she eagerly returned my greeting with a nod and a *"Buenos días."* With my broken Spanish I told her that the floor looked beautiful, and she was happy to hear that.

Just a few words, and I was able to encounter Jesus. I wanted this woman to be connected, to be part of the whole. I saw Jesus in her.

I also became thankful for my taste buds that allowed me to enjoy the banqueting table that my Lord provided. I never enjoyed food before Jesus took ownership of my taste buds—maybe because I never thanked Him for the food. I always dove in like a dog without recognizing that my food was a gift from God to nourish my body. I started taking time to taste my food, to thank God for it and to enjoy it purposely. Jesus was even changing my taste buds.

My tongue was created to bless, to encourage, to build people, and to speak well of God and of others. Most of all it was made to praise Him, the only One who is worthy. Jesus, God of my tongue.

* * * * *

Jesus taught my nose to smell a fresh-brewed cup of coffee in the morning, the fragrance of the flowers, the sweet-scented, well-fed ground after the rain, and the forest that reminds me of spring and summer. These things caused praise to rise within my soul.

My Jesus also helped me to smell the disinfectant and the rubbing alcohol in a hospital, which reminded me of sick people, and He allowed me to smell the decaying body of a dying person—"the sting of death" (1 Corinthians 15:56). This taught me to cry for fallen humanity and for the magnitude of what death has done. It drove me to the cross in intercession and gave me a heart that is thankful for the resurrection.

I also became thankful that my nose allowed me to breathe and helped sustain me. Jesus, God of my nose.

* * * * *

All of us come to Jesus having some idea of what we are going to get when we give our lives to Him. My idea was that I was forgiven. I thought I could just slap Jesus on my forgiven self and go to work for Him. But I did not know that when I slapped Jesus on my forgiven self, He would have the tendency to get under my skin and penetrate my innermost being.

It's like a tissue graft on a burn victim—the tissue is absorbed into a new part of the body, and it becomes one with that part. So in the same way I started to become like Him. I absorbed Him. As I studied the Word, prayed, and worshiped, my mind was being renewed, my senses heightened, my values changed. My thoughts were becoming Jesus' thoughts.

Years earlier, I had voted for Clinton; now I voted Republican. It was an inside job. I no longer was subject to the daily changes of the world or the news. I was experiencing freedom!

I discovered too that loving people unconditionally was a choice. I had to choose to have no ill or evil thoughts toward anyone, and not only that, but to have good thoughts toward them as well. I did not have to agree with them or ever associate with them, but I had to be always ready to help people and extend the scepter of grace to them and pray for them. Then I could let God do what was required and leave all judgment to Him.

Now liking is a matter of taste. Liking someone means that we have an affinity for them. We like the way we feel around that person; we agree on things. But liking and feeling happy with people are subject to change, whereas love is eternal.

I learned to have love and joy in Jesus, and as I shared His love with others, I received more. Love does not work when we keep it to ourselves. In fact, it ceases altogether.

* * * * *

So we honor God with our eyes by abstaining from anything that does not glorify Him. We honor Him with our ears by listening to what is good and acceptable—the Word of God, praise music, the words of others who have a heart for God. We honor Him with our senses by refusing to use them wrongly and offering them to Him for His use.

I had not arrived; my daily struggles of walking with God remained. I still had moments when the flesh, Satan, and the world harassed me, but my recovery became much quicker, and getting up became easier. Just as with running, Jesus built my endurance so that breathing Him in would become effortless.

Little by little, my feelings became more tender and more secure, my emotions more balanced, my thought process more in line with God. I learned patience with God and with people. My decisions became rational. I was amazed at how God was changing me in every area of my life. It was as if I was becoming another person.

I enjoyed the invisible God being visible in my life not only because of what He had done but also because of what He had given me: life. My mind, my heart, and even my physical body were the sanctuary of the living God, and He always sanctifies His sanctuary.

I loved having pure thoughts in the process of spiritual homeostasis—the process of becoming spiritually balanced. When a thought came into my mind, it went through the filter of the Holy Spirit, and He brought to my conscience any thought that was not from Him. The moment I agreed with God, the thought dissipated immediately.

My God became the God of my senses as He took control of my mind (the center of my intellect) and my heart (the center of my emotions). As He permeated my senses, He revived my spirit, which had been dead.

My senses began to experience redemption. I had a heightened awareness of my true self, where Jesus resided. The world around me became vibrant. My taste, smell, sight, hearing—all my senses were balanced. I became an eternal optimist, full of hope. I was in a broken world, and yet my world was whole and full of peace.

My ears heard the joyful sounds of His praises and the painful sound of a world that was out of tune with Him. He helped me to hear both the joy and the pain. He taught my ears to listen with compassion.

My eyes saw His creation—the vast sea, the mountains, the trees, the flowers, and even the desert, which reminded me of a broken planet groaning for His redemption. I also saw the suffering of humanity—a frail body, a mother holding her hungry child and asking with her eyes if I could help. He showed me the beauty but also the pain and the suffering, which at times were hard to look at. But He beckoned me to see. He looked at people through my eyes so that He could connect with the world, one person at a time, with compassion, love, and mercy.

And since my senses were still capable of being used by the flesh, the world, and Satan, I thanked God for His grace that covered my shortcomings.

10

LEARNING FREEDOM AND SIMPLICITY IN JESUS

I fear, lest somehow, as the serpent deceived Eve by his craftiness, so your minds may be corrupted from the simplicity that is in Christ.
2 Corinthians 11:3

As I became more subject to the Holy Spirit, He began to deal with me on issues like nationality, religion, color, gender, social and financial status, and political preference. He clearly showed me how pride can clothe itself in any of these titles. I was not to ignore them or pretend that they did not exist, but I needed to cultivate a healthy attitude toward God's awesome creation and His artistic work in people. We are all equal in the eyes of the Lord with no pride or prejudice.

God freed me from these things and allowed me to see with the eyes of Jesus.

I had been restored to God through the death and resurrection of Jesus Christ; I now had everything in Christ. I had been born into a new life. I now had to bring everything under subjection to the new life.

I came to see that in Jesus I no longer lived under the coverings of culture, nationality, religion, color, gender, and social status. These were all rooted in pride and covetousness, which is a coat of many colors.

Covetousness results when we are not satisfied with what we are given. Christians are tempted to covet material things, as the world is, comparing houses, cars, clothes, neighborhoods. We are tempted as well to covet position regarding race, social status, gender, and other things. But besides all that, we tend to covet spiritual things.

We compare our spiritual gifts with the gifts that God has given other believers, and we covet what others have. For example, God may have given someone the gift of helps, but that person covets the gift of teaching that God has given a sister or brother. So instead of thanking God for the saints who have the gift of teaching and also thanking Him for our own gift of helps (or compassion or hospitality or mercy or kindness), we are dissatisfied. Everybody should be content with his or her spiritual gifts, and if we want more gifts, we ought to ask God, who gives liberally (see James 1:5).

The competitive American spirit has slipped in the back door of the church too, wearing this multi-colored garment of comparison and covetousness, causing some believers to covet positions of power and influence. But Christians are not called to be at the top the way Americans try to be. In the church it is God who calls us into leadership. We don't strive to lead; leadership is given to us by God.

Christians also compare churches. A woman once told me that if I did not attend a certain church, I was not a real Christian.

The Lord showed me that comparing myself with others was a deadly spiritual game to play, because it would cause me to lose the joy of the Lord. Not only that, but it was clearly telling God that He had not done a good enough job with what He had given me or where He had placed me. I was chosen and beloved by God, who knew my needs and gave me the spiritual gifts and position that were suitable for the body of Christ. What He gives us is for the benefit of others, so whatever we have, we must use it without covetousness.

The multi-colored coat of covetousness is made up of pride, greed, idolatry, comparison, competition. But at its root, covetousness is really none other than insecurity as to who we are in God and who God is. When we covet, we are saying, "I don't believe what God says about me, and equally, I don't believe that this God, Jesus, who holds the universe in His hands, is capable of holding me and caring for me." This is unbelief, a lack of faith. And without faith, we cannot please God.

When we compare ourselves with others, we end up competing with them, trying to get closer to God by doing more for Him than someone else is. We fail to see that God could never love us more than He did on the day we were born. We do well when we accept our own gifts and talents as well as each other's and know that Jesus is enough.

Heavenly Father, in the name of Jesus, may You be enough.

* * * * *

I do not believe that as a rule Christians covet things in a mean-spirited way; in our hearts we truly love God and desire to please Him. But we get busy *doing* things for God, while God is saying, "Simply follow Me, simply stay connected, simply abide, and I will give you instructions to guide you and bless you." Easy, right?

Christianity is believing, feeling, seeing, and absolutely knowing the invisible God. That is radical—but *He* is radical. We will never know Him unless we ask Him to reveal Himself to us in sincerity and truth. He changes us from within and promises to do so.

When we are connected to God, we have a bendable heart and bended knees.

In this world we will always have covetousness—the coat of many colors: pride of self, religion, nationality, color, country, zip code, gender. The ugliness of covetousness and pride always gives birth to comparison and competition, but as Christians (followers of Christ) and as a church (called-out ones) we need to be aware of this pitfall of Satan, who uses our personalities and the things of the world to rob us of our freedom and simplicity in Christ. We need to perceive with our spiritual eyes this hindrance, which keeps us from the enjoyment of our faith.

This is a continuous endeavor in our walk with Christ.

I lived in a number of countries before I settled in the U.S., and I must say that I never saw a country as competitive and busy trying to measure up as America. No wonder Americans are the best in everything—people are killing themselves to be top dog.

People in other countries where I lived didn't have the chance to get to the top, for there was always a family or two that ruled due to monarchy or dictatorship or a class or caste system that thwarted people in their efforts to get ahead. So the common man learned to be content with his loaf of bread and jug of wine or with his bowl of rice or beans or corn or hummus and tabouli with tea. Even though these countries have seen gross injustice and inequality, which is abominable, sometimes I wondered who slept better at night—them or us.

It is good that Americans have the freedom to succeed and rise to the top. Working hard to get ahead is not bad. I simply wondered when having enough was enough.

When I first came to America, people asked me, "Aren't you glad you're here?"

Umm, no, I thought. *I'm a hostage here . . .*

But Somali people were no less prideful. I came from a proud culture. Our people were resilient, independent. We were nomads and went wherever we wanted—no restrictions. We had a code of honor; a person's word was his bond. People had no hidden agendas. These qualities my people loved and valued, and so did I.

But in Jesus I had to lay to rest who I thought I was. That did not diminish my Somali heritage, of course. I was thankful for my country, my family, my childhood. But without Jesus we are nothing. So I lost it all—and gained so much more.

* * * * *

I saw many beautiful pictures of Christ's simplicity and His love for people of every kind when I began running.

In my late forties, I developed an affinity for running. I had loved to run as a child, but when I came of age, which is about twelve to thirteen years old, running had been put to a stop, because it was not culturally appropriate in my country for girls to run. So at the age of forty-nine, I started running a mile or two. I went on eventually to run a half marathon, and I started training with the hope of running a marathon at age fifty. Sad to say, I got hurt one week before the marathon, and I was not able to run. Nevertheless, my love for running continued, and nowadays, at the age of fifty-eight, running is my pastime.

Jesus ran with me. Running truly became a passion of mine, because it was so fitting for talking to Jesus heart to heart. I was awake, my mind was alert, my spirit receptive—it was just fun to run with Jesus. It's not that I imagined Him; He was actually with me. We talked about everything, we cried, we laughed, we thought through things. He gave me plans for my day; He refreshed me. I found myself praising Him and giving Him thanks for my legs, my eyes, my ears, my mind, and my heart, which is my Jesus' home. I enjoyed Him so much that when my plan was to run five miles, I ended up running seven or more simply because I was with Jesus. No iPhone or iPod, just me and Jesus. I felt the wind, I heard the birds, I saw the trees swaying, and in those moments I was one with Jesus and His creation. In my world everything was in its place.

I became part of a beautiful community of walkers, runners, and some cyclists. When I encountered any of them,

I always raised my right hand—my way of imparting peace and blessing to them. They almost all responded with a smile, a nod, a word, or a raised hand. Cyclists were difficult to connect with, maybe because of their speed or their intensity. I prayed that they would experience the joy of the Lord. I blessed everyone—young, old, male, female, homeless. After all, it was Jesus who was greeting them, and He loved all of them.

One day I told Jesus, "Lord, You are getting me into trouble with this raising of my hands to bless everyone. It might be misinterpreted, especially with males or unbalanced people."

I heard Him in the rhythm of my heart saying, "Maryama, in My world there is no male or female. And what are you afraid of? I am here, right? Would you deny someone blessing because you are afraid of what he or she might think?"

I was ashamed. "Oh Lord, You know all things," I remarked sheepishly. "It's a good thing that I am dark skinned, because You cannot see me blushing."

"I made your dark skin, and yes, I see you blushing," Jesus remarked.

One morning as I ran, I saw a homeless man sitting in a corner by the river trail. He seemed tired and weary as he looked down, all his worldly belongings beside him. As I was about to pass, I raised my hand of blessing and uttered, "Good morning." He looked out in amazement with his beautiful green eyes and a toothless smile that lit up the world. "Good morning," he replied.

Something, or Someone, touched my soul deeply that moment. That homeless man blessed me immeasurably. I had simply said good morning to him, but that day someone had thought he was worthy of being acknowledged. Someone had noticed that he was there and part of the whole. He mattered. And I was the recipient of the beautiful smile of a toothless homeless man who bore the eyes of Jesus. He had a broken and unkempt body, but his eyes were full of life and light.

I whispered to my Lord, "Oh, sweet Jesus, how is it that I feel blessed by this homeless man?"

"I am in Him," was His reply. "I am with the broken, downtrodden, marginalized, poor. That is where I am mostly found." Glorious!

* * * * *

For seven years I was in the classroom of Jesus, learning and understanding who He was and what He required of me—that He died so that He could infuse His very life into me. It was a tremendous growth period of getting hold of what it means to be a Christian. I was like a blank page, and Jesus was writing His story in me.

I'd had no basis or foundation or any clue as to what Christianity was, but the way Jesus revealed Himself through the Word, prayer, meditation, and the sweet fellowship of believers was truly something to behold. I was becoming a different person. I was in awe over everything—life, people, nature. Everything seemed new.

My past was fading. I had a difficult time sometimes remembering that I was from Somalia. At times I had a hard time knowing who I really was. I felt as if Someone else was living in me, but I happily yielded to Him.

Trials came, and I would be jolted back to my past and stay in the mire for a while as if I was stagnant. But I continued to keep what I had received, for it was a pearl of great price. Jesus taught me to trust Him in trials and difficulties, because He was my Shepherd.

Mostly the first seven years were like a honeymoon. Jesus shepherded me gently; He provided, He protected, He loved. Oh, how I thank Him! I had accepted Him as the God of eternity, but I had discovered later that He was the God of the here and now for me as well. This was truly too much for me to take. I wept and profusely thanked Him. Sometimes I was speechless, and all I could utter was "Lord, You are too much." I had no way of thanking Him appropriately, and I feel the same way today. I love Him.

11

MEETING MY SOUL MATE

Marriage is honorable among all.
Hebrews 13:4

My life with Jesus was blossoming; I needed nothing but Him.

He had blessed me in every way. I was flourishing in my work, enjoying holistic massage, and I had been able to buy a beautiful home in Laguna Hills. My daughter had gone to college on the East Coast, and my son was doing well in high school. I had rich fellowship with other believers and continued to grow in my faith.

One summer afternoon in 2000, I was shopping in a health-food store owned by a Lebanese Christian. I often frequented the shop. The owner was always kind enough to talk with me about Jesus, and this also enabled me to brush up on my poor Arabic skills. This man helped me incorporate and harmonize my Christian faith with Middle Eastern culture.

As I was leaving the store that day, a man walked in. He surprised me by immediately demanding that it was too soon for me to leave—after all, he had just met me. I looked back at the owner in a puzzled way, wondering who this crazy guy was. The owner gave me a look of assurance that the man was harmless. Meanwhile, this guy blocked my way at the door and finally asked me kindly if I would have a smoothie with him if I had the time.

I happened to have the time. It was a Saturday afternoon, Eric was visiting Eda on the East Coast, and nothing about my day was urgent. So I agreed to have a smoothie with him in the store. I felt safe, for I was in a public place, and my friend the owner was there.

We talked awhile, and this guy, whose name was Ken, asked if he could take me to dinner sometime. I told him I was married. He was embarrassed, and I immediately clarified, "I am married to Jesus. Are you a Christian?"

He replied sarcastically, "Of course I am a Christian—I am an American from Indiana." I believed him, because I did not know the difference between a cultural Christian and a true lover and follower of Jesus. He continued, "Listen, this is a crowded place. There is a park at Mesa Verde—do you mind if we take a walk or sit on a bench so we can talk?" Since I had no pressing matter to attend to, I agreed. He gave me his business card, and before I left, I checked with my friend the owner of the store. He assured me that this guy was safe. So I went to the park to meet Ken.

But he was not there. It happened that he had been talking about a different park—and we missed each other. So we had lost each other forever—or had we? Remember, I had his business card, although he did not have mine. So he just had to wait for me to call.

The number was for his office (this was in the days before smartphones), so he went to his office, and I went home and waited awhile. I did not think that he had ditched me but rather that there had been some error in the directions. So I called, and he answered immediately.

We talked about the deep stuff of life like "What kind of food do you like?" We talked about our failed relationships, about what the other person had done to us or not done, and about how, of course, nothing had been our fault. Finally we agreed to dinner one week from that day, which was really a God thing. It gave us a chance to dig a little deeper in conversation before we met again. We talked every night before our date, and I noticed a strength in Ken that was attractive to me.

* * * * *

Our dinner date was at an Angels baseball game. We met at the health-food store and went to the game together from there. Ken had season tickets for Club Level, next to the press box. We had dinner at the club. I do not remember much about the game, but it was a beautiful evening. We came back to where my car was, and I left for home. He did not know where I lived, and that was okay.

Ken and I talked every night that week. The conversation was more toward God than us. I asked him about the church he attended, and he told me that he had grown up in the church but had left when he came of age. But he would love to go with me to church, he said. So I invited him to a Christian concert in a tent at the Orange County fairgrounds.

But first I told him that I was not interested in dating a non-Christian. Ken told me that he had grown up in a Christian home and at one time had thought he was a Christian, but his father had been physically abusive, and when Ken came of age, because of condemnation and guilt it had been easy for him to leave the church. But he had a Christian mom who had loved him and never given up on him, and he was willing to give God a second chance.

I told him that Jesus is not like what he knew of Him. He was kind, patient, and loving—a forgiving God, a giving God, a merciful and gracious God. He was strong and mighty, He healed and restored, He mended relationships, and He gave peace. He was a good God.

We went that evening to the Christian revival concert, and this was the first time that Ken heard contemporary Christian music. The words and the instruments touched him deeply. He loved the bass.

The gospel was presented in a clear, simple manner, and the last song was an invitational. One of the singers sang, "All who are thirsty, all who are weak, come to the fountain." When my future husband heard that song, the Holy Spirit fell upon him, and he was born again that day.

This was not the Christianity he had grown up with. His spirit was awakened; he was given a new heart—a new Ken was born! He was enlightened. He loved the worship songs.

He had grown up with hymns and been told that music with drums and guitars was considered evil.

I wondered if they had read Psalm 150: "Praise Him with the sound of the trumpet; praise Him with the lute and harp! Praise Him with the timbrel and dance; praise Him with stringed instruments and flutes! Praise Him with loud cymbals; praise Him with clashing cymbals!" (150:3–5).

* * * * *

Even though we were mature in our chronological age, both Ken and I were young in the faith. But we knew one thing for sure: we loved Jesus, and we loved one another. Shortly after this Ken proposed to me and asked to marry me right away, but our Jesus said not yet. My son, Eric, and Ken's son, Matt, were away for the summer, and when we shared the good news of our meeting with them, it was not good news to them.

Eda was okay with the idea of me marrying after she flew home and met Ken. But both of our sons were entering their second year in high school and had a lot of changes taking place in their lives. Eric was growing in his faith, but the changes were too much for a young mind, and he told me tenderly that he needed me now and did not want me to marry. Ken's son shared the same sentiment with him. Both our sons were very good boys, but they were young and vulnerable, and changing their environment could have been detrimental to their growth. Ken and I talked about it, and we decided to hold off on marriage for the boys' sake.

What we did not know was that our Jesus had His hand in all these events. Even though we were new creations in

Christ and loved each other, He wanted us to grow in His love, not the world's love, which says, "I will love you as long as I like you." Since we were young in the faith, loving in the world's love and loving in God's love were one and the same to us. How to differentiate the two was not clear to us—it was just one word—"love."

Our Lord's intention was to separate the two kinds of love for us so that we could love one another in God's love, which is more excellent and more enduring and more wholesome. So we entered a new paradigm.

God began digging deeply into our souls to heal and restore us from the past. We were two broken, battered souls who were new creatures in Christ but holding in our memory banks hurt and betrayal, broken promises, disloyalties, dishonor, lies. These had birthed anger, grief, loss, unforgiveness, and distrust, which had brought about defensiveness, pride, fear, pretense, insincerity, selfishness, and the like.

You may think, *Those things were done to you*, and maybe so. But our Lord was dealing with *us*. Both the wrongs done to us and those things we had done to others had to be all forgiven. We had to be healed from them and then restored. Our new relationship was so precious to our Lord that He saw fit to deal with our past, for there would be enough troubles and trials to come without dragging our past into our new relationship.

Dealing with the past was not easy or comfortable for me. I can truly say that it was painful. Especially hard was facing my failures and shortcomings, my temper and fears.

I had always held others responsible for my failures. I loved people as long as I liked them and they liked me, and as long as they were beneficial to me in one way or another. But as soon as there was conflict, I was done. And of course it was always the other person's fault—not once was it mine.

People had indeed hurt me, but my Lord was interested in showing me first the part that I had played in any situation so that I could make an honest assessment of the past. Only then could I have a happy, joyful future.

So I began therapy sessions with Jesus. It started in my morning meetings with Him. Each day I started with worship and thanksgiving. I read the Word and meditated on it, and I prayed for the kids and Ken and whomever God put on my heart. Then I quieted my mind to hear what the Lord had to say to me. *Pop!* Something from the past, always unpleasant and stressful, came up, and He asked me to forgive someone or to forgive myself. Each struggle went on for a week or more. Talk about wrestling with God.

I started each struggle with denial. Imagine my gall— trying to straighten out the all-knowing God about how He misunderstood the whole thing or how it was not that serious or how that was not how it had all gone down.

Then came anger and shame followed by remorse and guilt.

Lots of tears fell in those years of purging. The shower became a haven for me—I would put the fan on and start the shower so that no one would hear me, and I would start wailing. After my weeping, I would finally come to the place of owning what had happened, and I would take it to the cross. Each time I told Jesus, "Lord, this is what I did," or,

"Here is what I believe was done to me." Then I told Him, "I do not know how to forgive this person, for the hurt is deep," or, "I do not know how to forgive myself, because I feel ashamed." I asked Him, "Here it is—would You help, if You are willing? I do not want to be enslaved or held hostage by bitterness and unforgiveness anymore. I want my heart to be Yours."

I wept for my past; I wept for the years I had not known my Jesus; I wept for the wrongs that had been done to me and the wrongs that I had done, real or imagined. I wept for the wasted years of living a meaningless life.

These struggles went on for a long time. With each one I faced a different event from my past, but the cycles of dealing with each struggle were the same—denial, anger, bargaining, then remorse. You would think that I would have learned the first or second time and would have just brought the past to Jesus immediately when something came up and let Him help me. But my sweet Jesus continued to purge me, and I can honestly say that every event from my past was dealt with at the cross.

I think the Lord was up to something in letting me go through the stages of grief. You see, it's easy to gloss over things quickly, to forgive easily and quickly without really thinking through the ramifications of what exactly has happened and how deep the hurt has been.

God forgave us, and His forgiveness is free to us, but what God did in order to forgive us and restore us to Himself was not cheap. A heavy price was paid on our behalf. So too when we forgive someone, if indeed we genuinely forgive, it costs us tremendous pain. But that is when Jesus steps in and helps us forgive without any strings attached.

Some of you might say, "Are we not already forgiven for every offense of our life, past, present, and future?" You are right—we are indeed forgiven. But I am talking about forgiving others and forgiving ourselves in order that our prayers and our fellowship with God will not be hindered.

You see, it is hard to enjoy God and have sweet fellowship with Him and His people when we are holding unforgiveness and bitterness in our heart, which is actually Jesus' home. Imagine our Lord entering a place of bitterness, clamor, and unforgiveness and making it His home. Think about that for a moment. So yes, we are forgiven by Jesus, but He gives us a chance to reconcile or restore things where possible. That is another advantage of forgiving—mending and restoring relationships.

Of all the parts of the grief process, the two most ridiculous are denial and bargaining. Denial is lying to God about what happened and saying that His evaluation of it is not right. Bargaining is going to church seven days a week, hoping it will go away; but God is all knowing, and He is the One who did everything to forgive and cleanse us so that all we have to do is bring everything to Him who says, "I am willing."

The cycle of denial, bargaining, remorse, and acceptance continues in my life, but the duration is getting shorter. These issues visit me again and again, because we live in a fallen world with our imperfect self and with imperfect people.

So Ken's and my plans for marriage were put on hold while our boys enjoyed high school with all its growing pains and our daughter experienced the growing pains of a young adult in her early twenties. Ken and I were in a holding stance. God was doing a tremendous work in our hearts. We were learning that we were forgiven and learning how to forgive others in God's way.

* * * * *

The boys graduated from high school and went to college, Eric in Southern California, a couple hours from home, and Matt in Vermont. It was hard to be empty nesters, but most of all I was fearful of Eric falling away from his faith. Eda was on her way to being an apostate, and each year her faith was getting weaker, so my concern for Eric was great, even though we had switched to a strong Bible-teaching church while he was in high school, and he had a firm grasp of his faith.

Before he went to college, I told him that his faith was no longer his mother's but his own. "No one will tell you when to pray, go to church, or read the Bible," I told him. "You are on your own, my son. Live a quiet and peaceful life, and find a way to stay connected to Jesus and the body of Christ. And I will pray."

God was faithful to Eric and showed His kindness to me. He led Eric to a group of Christians at the campus, and for four years he stayed connected with his faith in a secular university, and he reaped great friendships and faithful brothers for life. He studied one semester in Berlin, Germany, and managed to connect with a believer there as well.

* * * * *

After the boys went to college, Ken and I were ready to tie the knot, but it was not time yet according to Jesus. We faced one hurdle after another. Ken's business burned to the ground. Then his father died.

But we kept growing in our relationship with God and with each other. Seven years passed, and we never had a doubt that we were right for each other, even when we had heated arguments. We did not cross any lines. We talked every night. Kenny came faithfully every Sunday to take me to church; we had lunch and took walks together, and he went home. We remained faithful to each other and to Jesus.

When Ken's business burned down, it was a big blow, but amazingly Ken remained calm and peaceful. In fact, he was so calm that the investigators thought that he had set the fire. When they found out that he did not have insurance, they were confused and did not know what to make of him. I am not sure if they figured out that he was a Christian. With God's grace and mercy, Ken recovered quickly.

Finally we set the day for our wedding—May 11, 2007.

Ken asked me how my new house was to look. "I want the downstairs to be one great room," I told him. "I want the living room, sitting room, dining room, and kitchen all in one room so that everybody will be in one place when they visit us. Our house will be the house of feasting where everyone who comes will be refreshed." Open, like our hearts, is what I wanted our house to be. Open to God and open to people—a house of blessing. I told Ken that I wanted a fountain in the front yard and one in the back. They would remind us of the spring of living water in us—our new life in Christ.

Eda designed the house, and Ken built it, including our furniture.

The day of the wedding came. I did not have to do anything. Ken arranged everything—the wedding planner, the make-up and the hair lady. When I had explained to Ken that Somali weddings are always arranged by the groom, he told me that that's what he would do. And he did.

My daughter was my bridesmaid, and my Jesus provided the perfect dress. It was a wedding arranged by my Father, God.

I checked in at the Hotel Laguna the night before my wedding and had dinner with the kids. The wedding took place the next afternoon on the terrace of the Hotel Laguna. Nothing was spared, all the way to the last detail. Our kids entered into the covenant with us; it would be a family affair through thick and thin.

We went to Santa Barbara for our honeymoon. Afterward I moved to my new home with Ken and rented my beautiful cottage in Laguna Hills. Thus seven years of courting came to a happy ending.

PART 3

SHINING IN A DARK WORLD

12
TRIALS OF LIFE

Weeping may endure for a night, but joy comes in the morning.
Psalm 30:5

Ken and I settled into married life with ease. Well, mostly. We ended up having the first fight of our marriage on our honeymoon.

It started when Ken asked me to sign a paper stating that his company would stay with him in case a divorce visited us. I was crushed and bewildered. But strangely enough, my anger was not directed to Ken but to my Shepherd. You see, I had not asked for this relationship; I had been perfectly happy to be alone with my Shepherd and totally satisfied doing life with Him. But I had fallen in love with this guy, and now he was asking me to do this unspeakable thing. Where did divorce fit into our story?

I thought I had been tricked. I wanted to run away as I had before—but now the back door was closed. I started to weep. Once again I felt the presence of the Shepherd, and I told Him that I wanted to run away. He replied, "You cannot run emotionally anymore, but you can run physically, and we will talk about the matter."

So I started to run, pounding the ground. After about two miles I found my rhythm, and I started to calm down. My anger subsided, and the Lord broke through. First He showed me Ken's fears and how he had been devastated and lost everything in his first divorce. Then He reassured me that I should go ahead and do what my husband was asking me to do.

That was tough to take. But it came back to the question, did I trust my Jesus?

So yes, I signed that silly document, and yes my marriage is everlasting. Today I am in love with Kenny more than ever before and in love with Jesus more than yesterday.

The difficulty on our honeymoon notwithstanding, the years of cultivating our relationship with God's wise counsel paid off. Our kids were grown and doing well. Kenny's son came to work for him after he graduated from college, Eda returned from the East Coast to Southern California, and Eric went to law school and found his home in Portland, Oregon. So it was just my Ken and me at home, doing life together with Jesus.

We were thankful for the way God had grounded us in Him, because one year after our marriage, Ken was diagnosed with prostate cancer. It was confirmed through a biopsy. We tried a diet change and herbal medicine, to no avail. It was a difficult time for us, because we were newlywed, just one year into marriage. We mourned together, but my husband remained strong and full of hope. He assured me that he would not leave me. I clung to that hope. We decided to go ahead with brachytherapy, a type of radiation, which was less invasive than surgery. The treatment was successful, and we dodged the bullet. Praise and glory to our God!

Ken has been in remission since then. The radiation took a lot out of him, and he still suffers fatigue and low energy, but I thank God for his life. God has shown His kindness to us.

* * * * *

After Ken's treatment he sent me and Eda for R & R to Paris. It was a great gift. My daughter and I flew first class to Paris and spent ten days there.

When we came home, I came down with a bad flu. A week later things got worse—I developed Bell's palsy. The right side of my face was paralyzed, my right eye unable to close. It was devastating. My beautiful face would never be the same. For three months I had to cover my right eye to protect it. I could not work with one eye covered, and I could not drive. My speech was impaired as well. I mourned my loss, and my husband mourned with me.

I felt distance from the Lord, whether real or imagined. I truly had to examine myself and discern whether God was upset with me or I was hearing the words of the enemy.

In the following weeks, when I got up each morning and realized that the Bell's palsy was still with me, I went back to bed, devastated with grief. Sometimes I lay on the floor weeping. All this time I did not blame God once—I just wanted to know if He was still with me and if there was a meaning in all this.

After about three months of this, one morning I was facedown in my usual place on the floor, and I wept bitterly. Finally my crying turned into a soft whimper, and my whimpering became quieter and quieter. At that moment I felt a heaviness come upon me, as if someone had put a thick blanket on me. It was so comforting. I had never felt this safe before, and I was comforted in this peaceful place. I drifted off to sleep. About two hours later I woke up refreshed and not caring about Bell's palsy anymore. That day I surrendered. "Not my will but Yours, oh Lord," was my response.

That morning after having this encounter with God and experiencing His presence, love, affection, and care for me, I mentioned to God how I missed running. With one eye my depth perception was compromised—I saw flat ground where there was a dip or a dip where it was flat, and I would trip, so it was difficult for me to run. But that morning, clear as a bell, Jesus told me to run. I immediately put on my running gear and went out the door without any hesitation. Amazingly, I ran for about an hour with smooth flowing strides and did not trip or fall. It was an incredible experience.

As I got to the gate of my house, I said to myself, *Wow, I did it!* At that moment I tripped and fell on my face. I was reminded that it was my Jesus who had given me this beautiful experience, and I had robbed Him of His glory. I repented and worshiped the Lord.

I took a long shower that morning. I was at a turning point in my relationship with God through the trials He had brought into my life. I began to realize that it is in the trials that we grow in the grace of God and that in those three months God had been dancing around me and singing over me. It was amazing.

Before I was a Christian, the trials of life had always made me bitter. But I noticed now that the trials of this life made me better. They helped me to relate to others and comfort them with the comfort I had been given.

We experience God's nearness when we are suffering, for He is a caring God. I love experiencing God when trials come, and they always come. Every one of us is either going through a trial or has just come through a trial or has a trial on its way. When things are going well, we must learn to build our foundation on Christ so that when the rains and the storms come, we will stand on the rock, Jesus.

* * * * *

So I called my doctor and told him that I was ready to go back to work. He examined my eye and was impressed with how healthy it looked. By God's wisdom I had taken good care of it by covering it and putting ointment on it to keep it moist.

My healing was a process, but it began when I stepped out in faith. I began driving to work with one eye, praying before and after each trip for the Lord's protection over me and others on the road. Not only did He grant it, but He also gave me the privilege of experiencing His presence. His glory filled the car. At times I wept for joy, and all I could say was "Holy, holy, holy." It was a very special time with God in my deficiency. My healing started with my eye; then my speech returned, and my face corrected somewhat.

I still have evidence of the Bell's palsy, but I am grateful for the growth I experienced and am still experiencing. Smiling is hard for me—my facial nerves send an incorrect signal that makes it look as if I am frowning or about to cry. It seems sad, but it is glorious indeed. Also, the wind irritates my face, so I have to stay away from windy places, which is not conducive to my hiking, running, or any outdoor activities, which I very much enjoy. But I press forward and tolerate the irritation, remembering the short days I have in this life. I want to live to the limit without any hindrances.

During the three months I was ill, I experienced God's loving-kindness and the love of His people. A letter that I wrote to my church shows how God's people cared for me:

Dear church,

Grace to you and peace from God our Father and the Lord Jesus Christ.

Your love and support have been amazing, and I thank God from the bottom of my innermost heart.

It has been nine weeks since my incident of Bell's palsy occurred, and the struggle continues. It has been the most challenging time in my life. Strangely enough, I have been through so much in my life that you might think that this would be a piece of cake, but on the contrary, the grief has been tremendous. One night I went to bed with everything the way it should be, and I woke up the next morning with life upside down— my speech, my sight, my taste, my smell, my laughter, my balance. Oh, don't forget my looks—vanity of vanities.

I started with disbelief, followed by a dose of denial; then discontentment with God laced with a touch of anger settled in where my Lord had before had complete ownership. I felt sick to my stomach, and my thoughts terrified me, then guilt overtook me, and I felt ashamed of my lack of faith. *Remember*, I told myself, *we are Christians; we are strong no matter what—keep a upper stiff lip*. But I was too weak to be strong.

In my weakness I continued to seek my Lord. I started to examine my life as the Word teaches, and I asked my Lord to reveal to me anything that was offensive to Him in my life. *He chose not to share*. Then I started to bargain, and I found out quickly that *He held all the cards*. I remembered people going through hard times who were still strong and happy, trusting the Lord, and I asked myself, *How do they do it? Would it be different if it was not on my face? Or am I this fake Christian who really never trusted the Lord?* That thought needed to be banished right away, because I knew that was not the truth.

You might be wondering if I have been seeking the Lord during this. The answer, my beloved, is affirmative—I have been praying, worshiping, and reading the Word more than I ever have. And I realized that God in His amazing wisdom chose to have His people minister to me. How comforting it has been to me for each one of you to pray, to call, to visit, to take me to doctors' appointments when hubby couldn't get away. Each one of you offered yourselves sacrificially, and even some of you blessed me with massages and facials. *How awesome is our God!* The Lord also brought other believers to minister to me, showing me again that we are one body regardless of our places of worship.

About the sixth week of this journey, we finished women's Bible study, and one of the sisters took me home. She mentioned thanking Him in everything, and it hit me like a ton of bricks—I had never thanked the Lord for this. I came home and sat down, and this tremendous grief came over me, and I wept bitterly. I couldn't bring myself to thank my beloved Lord for this. You see, this was an unfortunate thing, and giving thanks to my Lord meant that I was happy about this. I fell down on all fours and put my face on the floor and cried out, saying, "Lord, I don't know how to thank You for this. *Help me to thank You.*" I continued to weep, and I heard Him whisper, "It is okay to thank Me in grief." And then praise and worship with thanksgiving broke forth. I was still weeping but now it was joy mingled with *awe*. "What is this?" I asked. I have always known intimately the mercy of God, the love of God, the kindness of God, and I even knew His holiness, but nothing like this. I realized that in that position, facedown, I was before *a holy God*, and the option was to worship Him. Thanking Him in my situation continues to be a privilege.

The stories of Joseph and Job have been ministering to me. I know some of you might think that I am overstretching this because of the magnitude of Job's and Joseph's losses, but I thank my Lord that these stories are here for us, because, my beloved, grief and loss are relative things, and we suffer the same. Anyway, my struggle remains, but the Lord is with me, and my love for Him grows as He gives grace each day. I am learning to trust Him in a minute-by-minute walk, asking Him to consume me with His holiness. My prayer is, "Lord, purify me so that I can be a vessel fit for Your holiness," and I am patiently waiting for Him to heal me and to show me what that looks like.

Again, I thank the Lord for your love and support.

Shalom,

Maryama

* * * * *

Soon after my experience with Bell's palsy, Ken and I relocated to Calvary Chapel Costa Mesa. We had begun attending Calvary Chapel churches during the years we were dating and were so thankful that in these churches we had been grounded in the Word of God and in our knowledge of Christ. Now we were happy to be taught the Word by our beloved Pastor Chuck Smith and his son-in-law, Brian Brodersen. Cheryl Brodersen led the Joyful Life women's ministry.

Even in the trials of life, we were blessed.

13

THE CHRISTIAN PARADOX: LOSING EVERYTHING, HAVING ALL

Being found in appearance as a man, He humbled Himself and became obedient to the point of death, even the death of the cross.
Philippians 2:8

In 2010 my family announced the loss of my last worldly inheritance.

After my father's death and the civil war in Somalia in the 1990s, my family did not deal with the land inheritance. We had lost everything else—livestock and houses and other property. But Islamic law does not allow the land to be owned by another, and it still remained in our family, even though it was used and occupied by others without the family's consent.

So it finally came to pass that my family, along with the tribal elders, got together to divide the land. Sadly, I was not invited to be part of the meeting. Nor was I included in the inheritance. Since I was no longer a Muslim, not only did I lose my inheritance, but I was counted dead and not alive anymore. My last chance of being part of my family, country, and culture was dashed.

The reality of not belonging hit hard once again, and I mourned the loss. As I wept, I felt a familiar presence and heard a still, small voice saying, "I am your inheritance, and you are Mine." No longer was I part of the world I had known; no longer was I bound by shackles. I was free. I had lost my worldly inheritance—but I had gained Jesus.

My German American husband could not comprehend my grief, for I had two beautiful homes, one in Laguna Hills and one in Costa Mesa, and I was doing very well. Our kids were also doing well in life, and I had a loving husband and Jesus by my side. Yet I was grieving for being disowned and losing some dirt in war-torn Somalia.

I guess I was mourning for my identity. Somehow the foundation of who I was had been compromised. And yet does our Lord not require of us to find our identity not in self but in Him and Him alone? It took awhile for me to realize that there was a bigger plan in all this. I was being stripped and pruned so that I could bear much fruit. I had to learn to hold the world at a distance and Jesus close to my heart.

* * * * *

In Matthew 5 our Lord lays out the Christian paradox. He talks about how calamities come upon us as believers, yet we are blessed:

> Blessed are the poor in spirit, for theirs is the kingdom of heaven. Blessed are those who mourn, for they shall be comforted. Blessed are the meek, for they shall inherit the earth. Blessed are those who hunger and thirst for righteousness, for they shall be filled. Blessed are the merciful, for they shall obtain mercy. Blessed are the pure in heart, for they shall see God. Blessed are the peacemakers, for they shall be called sons of God. Blessed are those who are persecuted for righteousness' sake, for theirs is the kingdom of heaven.
>
> Blessed are you when they revile and persecute you, and say all kinds of evil against you falsely for My sake. Rejoice and be exceedingly glad, for great is your reward in heaven, for so they persecuted the prophets who were before you. (Matthew 5:3–12)

The world has trouble reconciling these amazing words of Jesus, and rightly so, because they have not met Jesus. But when we meet Him, really meet Him—not through the religious jargon of dos and don'ts but simply by coming to Him with empty hands and an open heart in faith—then things turn upside down, or, shall I say, right side up.

Of all the attitudes Jesus talked about, the one that I desire most and that is most difficult for me to gain is meekness. As I understand the word "meekness," it is not weakness but rather "power under control." It means valuing other people just as much as we value ourselves. Meek people are peacemakers. They don't insist on their rights but are always looking out for others, even sometimes at their own expense. When it comes to being right or being loving, they always choose being loving. They don't pursue self-interest but the interest of others; they have a forgiving heart. They absorb pain so that others may heal. Meekness is being with Jesus; it is choosing the Blesser instead of the blessing. It is the desire of every believer.

Meekness becomes more easily attainable as we mature in faith and develops as we go through trials and tribulations of life with Jesus. It matures when we experience mistreatment and adversity. We don't try to be meek—meekness comes to us through grace by Jesus Himself. Oh, how I desire that.

* * * * *

Christianity is illogical to the unregenerate world. It is not something anyone can explain. We simply enter in by faith in Christ Jesus. Then, once we do, a metamorphosis begins—we call this process of change sanctification. As I handled the loss of my family inheritance and my exclusion from the family circle, God was sanctifying me—changing me, teaching me, making me more like Him.

Sanctification is starting with one thing and ending up with something different, as when a caterpillar becomes a butterfly. Just as a caterpillar doesn't have what it takes to change itself into a butterfly, so I could not become sanctified by myself. It was God who was changing me from the inside out. This process is what the outside world sees and wonders about.

Once again I was reminded that we don't become holy by what we do but by the One who lives in us. Jesus and the Christian mingled together produce a different being, as each Christian becomes one with Him.

Christianity, as I understand it, is indeed a state of being. We are connected to and then continuously balanced by the God who created us for Himself, who says that we are the apple of His eye (see Zechariah 2:8). Truly Christian life is an unmovable, undisturbed, balanced life when our eyes are focused on the author and finisher of our faith—Jesus. As we live in a disturbed, broken, imbalanced world, those who are in Christ are in a state of homeostasis, a state of balance, and sustained by an invisible force—by Him whose name is Jesus. I found this to be so even in my grief and loss.

Before Jesus I was body, soul, and spirit. My *body* was in control, and I obeyed its needs and wants. My soul was led by my ego and my pride, and I was full of envy, war, covetousness, greed, gossip, and a competitive spirit. My spirit was dormant, with no strength or power to overcome evil or to do good.

As I opened my heart and cried out to God, Jesus invaded me, and all of a sudden inversion took place—I became spirit, soul, and body. The *spirit* now became the driving force of my life. It took control of my body and soul, and I became a new creation. Everything I was before was a contradiction to this new creation. What I am now is contrary to everything that this world expects or requires of me. So it is with each one who receives Jesus.

The new life is about being humble instead of prideful, being a lover instead of seeking love, being a giver instead of wanting to receive. When we are willing to give everything away, we gain much more. We seek mercy instead of vengeance, lose everything and yet win all, have nothing and yet gain everything. The new life is about losing self for others so that we can gain God and experience real self. It is a spirit-operated life, and if we try to do it in human ability, we lose it. It is a life filled with hope and adventure. It is about trusting God's love for us and loving others through Him. It is indeed a life of awe and wonder.

Losing my family inheritance gave me one more opportunity to learn this lesson. In this life I will never arrive at my final destination, but I am not worried about arriving. I am just enjoying doing life with Jesus in a world full of trouble and pain. I am busy loving others through Jesus, the One who gave me all.

* * * * *

I remembered how, when I was a child, my family had branded our livestock—every sheep, goat, cow, and camel was branded with the family seal. There was no question as to whom each animal belonged to; it was separated from other people's cattle. Sometimes several herds mixed with ours, and the livestock grazed together, but at the end of the day, the shepherds collected their own animals, because each one had the shepherd's seals of ownership.

It had hurt when my family excluded me from our inheritance, but I was comforted to know that I now had the seal of God (see Ephesians 1:13). My family seal was of the world, but my new seal, the Holy Spirit, confirmed that I was owned and led by my precious Jesus. Glorious!

Everybody in the world is branded. Which brand do you have? The world's brand and God's brand are diametrically opposed—we cannot have both. Either we have the seal of the world, or we have the seal of the Holy Spirit to live out the true Christian calling. If you are a Christian, you are owned by God and bear His seal, and thus the world recognizes that you are His.

* * * * *

Sadly, not every believer in Jesus experiences the joy of surrendering all to Him. Many try to add to Him, as I did when I was a young Christian. They are not content to lose everything to gain Jesus. They want more, like position, recognition, control, or religion. This is what we call a carnal Christian.

A carnal Christian to me is the most miserable thing to be, because carnal Christians do not believe that Jesus is enough. This attitude is rooted in the ugliness of pride, which entices Christians to live both in the church and in the world. Carnal Christians received Christ at one time in their life but somehow stopped growing in their faith, or they came to Christ seeking what they could get out of Jesus. They are always adding to Jesus—Jesus plus the world, Jesus plus status, Jesus plus religion. It is easy to spot a carnal Christian, because they are the unhappy Christians. Some have the martyr look; others think that God owes them.

They do all the religious duties and activities but lack the power to live for God. I believe that some carnal Christians were sincere in receiving Christ and are truly redeemed, but since they are not living only for God, they are missing out on the blessings and the rest that God has for them here and now. Carnal Christians make bad witnesses, and this is why the world does not see Jesus as He is. The light of these believers is hidden and the Spirit choked in them by the world's affairs, and God is not able to use them. They are Spirit quenchers, for they try to live the Christian life in their own strength instead of letting God's Spirit blossom in their hearts and refresh them so that they have true rest.

Unfortunately, carnal Christians fill the churches and are always looking for the next best thing to add to Jesus. They are work oriented. They are men pleasers instead of God pleasers. They love to read books about the Bible but not the Bible, and they seek blessing instead of the Blesser. When trials come, they blame God, for they always ask what God can do for them instead of asking for God Himself. They tend to be unstable and not sure of truth. They have difficulty accepting trials and hardship, and their faith fails them when these things come upon them.

Some Christians are carnal simply because they are new in the faith, and it is common to have a carnal mind when you are trying to learn about God. But staying carnal for ten, twenty, or thirty years and chasing after what one can add to Jesus is not only miserable but dangerous, because such believers misrepresent God.

* * * * *

Carnal Christianity has consequences, but God is gracious and merciful with awesome patience.

As I discovered earlier in my journey, our Lord Jesus came to this world with a specific agenda: to redeem humanity and to restore what we lost in the garden through disobedience. He came to reconnect us with God and to renew His original plan of man and God dwelling together forever and enjoying one another. He shed His blood on the cross and rose again so that we can enter into His rest and have sweet fellowship with God.

Why would we want more than that? Why wouldn't we be willing to give up everything, whether position or power or inheritance or family, in order to have Jesus?

I often wonder what He saw in me. Why would He yearn for me when He is so complete, perfect, and holy? Mystery of mysteries. But I am forever grateful, and there is not a day that I am not aware of His kindness that led me to repentance. I am so beside myself at being called His beloved!

So now, Christian friend, if you are not enjoying His rest, if you are trying to have Jesus plus something, then perhaps it is time to examine what you believe. There is nothing more that God can do and nothing you can add to what He's done.

Realizing that Jesus offers total forgiveness, put all your burdens down at the foot of the cross, where justice and mercy have kissed. It is time to stop meandering and to let go of anything that distracts you from Jesus. Enter His rest, and enjoy Him through worship, praise, and thanksgiving. When you do, He will guide you in all things and work His will through you each day. You will become pliable and bendable, and He will use you for His glory.

Carnality tries to please God through human will, emotion, intellect, and ego in order to gain God's love and affection, but it fails to recognize that this is a stench in God's nostrils. The spiritual man has a good understanding of the cross and of our utter helplessness and of the uselessness of trying to come to God in our own merits. It says, "I have nothing, yet I have everything in Christ." Selah!

Now that I have lost all my earthly inheritance, it is just Jesus and me, while I sow rich relationships with my husband, my children, and the body of Christ, especially my beloved sisters, who are many. Oh, how I cherish my relationship with Jesus.

My mantra is loving God and loving others—*the cross*. And in order to carry it out, I practice living the resurrected life—enjoying having nothing and yet owning everything. This is the paradox of being a Christian. We are in a state of homeostasis—balanced in the midst of pressure. I am learning to live in the agape love that seeks the wellbeing of others unselfishly and unconditionally.

Lord Jesus, forgive us for pretending to know You. Teach us to let go of the things that we think are so important and to find our rest in You so that we can truly love others. Help us to see that You really are enough.

14
SUFFERING AND FORGIVING

Forgive us our debts, as we forgive our debtors.
Matthew 6:12

In January of 2013, our own Pastor Chuck, whom we loved, was diagnosed with lung cancer. His sickness went on for many months, and we mourned as a congregation and as individuals while our pastor struggled and suffered. Even though Ken and I had never met him face to face, we found ourselves mourning for his pending departure. As his illness progressed, seeing him became painful. Since Pastor Chuck's illness affected all of us in the church, it revealed to me another dimension of our Christian life: when one suffers, we all suffer. We prayed for Pastor Chuck and his family and marveled at how our pastor's suffering affected us and at the mystery of how those in the body of Christ suffer with each other.

I remember Pastor Chuck's last sermon on September 29, 2013—he preached on Abraham's faithfulness. Our pastor was on oxygen; he was very weak, and every ounce of his energy was spent in simply saying a word or two. I found myself trying to breathe for him, and I noticed the people next to me doing the same thing. There were a lot of tears in the congregation. That Thursday, October 3, our beloved Pastor Chuck transitioned into eternity with God. He was God's friend, just as Abraham was.

I thanked God that the church had had a man of God who had been committed to God and to His Word. Now Pastor Brian, Pastor Chuck's son-in-law, was ready to take this generation on to the promised land.

In his later years Pastor Chuck reminded me of Moses. I saw him as a prophet; he gave a lot of warnings, as a prophet would. But Pastor Brian became a shepherd. He showed meekness and humility in the upheaval of the church. He was not afraid to take responsibility for the church and to bring the young and old together. We truly enjoy a healthy, vibrant church today that is experiencing the freshness of the Holy Spirit.

* * * * *

After Pastor Chuck's departure I faced yet another loss. I lost my job as a chaplain in a hospice company.

For fourteen years I had worked at a hospice company, caring for the dying and their families. I worked for seven years in holistic massage, and then in 2004, when my company eliminated my position, I was rehired by the company and trained to be a chaplain. This was a wonderful fit for me. My nursing and my holistic massage were both great assets to me; I understood the disease process and how it affects the whole person—physically, emotionally, and spiritually. That helped me in my chaplaincy, as I had a greater understanding of what patients were going through and how to walk through it with them. So even though I was never a nurse, my nurse's training had not gone to waste. In God's economy nothing is wasted.

My job as a chaplain had been a fruit-bearing ministry. Many of my clients and their families had tasted and seen God's goodness and His unfailing love for them. I had delivered God's message of love, grace, and mercy with tenderness and care. My intention had always been to bring people to God before their time came and to strengthen and encourage them and their families. I had tried to help them mend and restore relationships in the light of God's Word. I had shared Jesus in word and in deed with the simplicity of the gospel, the good news. It had been not a job but a ministry.

In late November 2013 I was called to the office by the director of patient care. The human resources person and my team leader were there. I was warned that dying people did not need to hear about Jesus or God, and I was asked to sign a paper stating that I would not tell people about Him.

This meeting took place because I had been lied about and accused of telling the patients that their cancer had been caused by God because of their disobedience to Him. Anybody who knows me knows that it is not like me to speak such things—to take the liberty of presuming to know why these people were suffering. These accusations hurt me deeply, and the thought of doing such a thing devastated me, because I truly loved and cared for each one of the patients and their families with the deep love of Christ, to the extent that I often felt their agony of grief.

The awesome thing is that I did not get angry but simply answered that the statements were not true. "I am a chaplain," I told them, "and I share spiritual things with the patients and their families only after I assess their spiritual needs and only after they give me permission to share the Word of God and pray with them and to impart blessing." With those who were not open to prayer, I went on, I offered simply to visit with them for support and encouragement, and I only prayed for them after I met with them, on my own.

In the days following this meeting, I was comforted by my Lord and stayed on course, having no offense toward my employers. I kept quiet and attended to my Father's business with grace and patience. I knew that I was to continue with God's plan, sharing Jesus with dying people and trusting Him with the results. I was convinced that whatever was going to happen, I was in good company and was safe because I knew Jesus.

After I was warned, God prompted me to get my affairs in order. My salary had been mainly for God; He used it according to His purpose, since my husband was capable of taking care of us, and our kids were all doing well, praise God. I had always had a heart for the persecuted church and for international missions, so my salary had become God's money with my husband's agreement. The first check always went to our local church, where we are blessed and taught the Word. I always paid this the first of the month, and in the middle of the month I gave to four different ministries and to others as the need arose.

I wrote the first check for the church, and I planned to pay the rest in the middle of the month, as usual. But God insisted that I pay the entire amount for the rest of the year, as well as the rest of my monthly giving, on the first of the month. I was surprised and pondered awhile. As a habit, when I receive an impression from God, I always wait for confirmation to make sure that it is from Him. This impression went on for three days, clear as a bell—God telling me to pay everything. So I agreed to what I was told by my Jesus. I started writing checks to finish the year, and I was up to date with all our ministries for the year 2013.

Then God visited me again and told me to give my only surviving uncle, who didn't have any kids and whom we supported, one year in advance instead of monthly. I did not wait for further confirmation, for I knew it was God, but I could not understand what He was up to. That's why He is who He is—God—and my place is to obey. So I did. All our obligation was given for the year.

On December 8, 2013, I was called to the office. It was about nine o'clock; I had already spent time with God and started my work that day. I told my superiors that I had two visits to make before I came. I knew that my time with the company was coming to an end. After I hung up the phone, I asked God to strengthen and prepare me for whatever was before me.

I visited the two patients and their families. I shared the gospel clearly, and the patients were receptive and blessed. Then I made my way to the office, and after a brief talk stating that the company now planned to cut back on my position, I was given a pink slip and let go.

The people who gave me the news told me that the decision had come from the top, and they cried and told me how I would be missed. I gave them tissues and encouraged them not to cry for me. I knew in my heart that whatever decision the company had made had passed through the filter of the Holy Spirit, and eventually it would be God's decision to bless or to indict this company for their actions. I prayed that God would show His mercy to them and that their letting me go would not be in vain but would be for His glory.

I felt the peace that I always feel when in distress, and I walked out of the office with Jesus. As I sat in my car, all of a sudden God revealed to me why He had pressed me to write the checks for the year: He had known what was coming and that I would have been insecure writing those checks after I was laid off, especially the one for a year's worth for my uncle. God was right! I would not have paid after losing the job. Oh, how He loves me. He did it for my protection—He knows my weakness.

My uncle, you see, had disowned me after I became a Christian, yet I always supported him. I gave the money to my sister to send to him and asked her not to mention that it was from me; otherwise he would not have accepted it. He was old, and I did not want to exasperate him, so Jesus provided for him. Amazing grace.

Losing my job was devastating in two ways: I lost a ministry, and I lost sixty thousand a year, which had been mainly used for God's kingdom.

I expressed this in a letter that I wrote to some of my closest sisters at church:

> Beloved sisters and longed-for friends,
>
> How often I think of you and your beloved ones, thanking and praising our beloved Savior and Lord for all He has done and is yet to do. Well, it has been a year of tremendous changes and growing pains, starting with our beloved Pastor Chuck departing to his eternal home and the Lord blessing us with a great man of God, our pastor Brian, with a great anticipation of what the Lord has for us. As He has said, "Be utterly astounded! For I will work a work in your days which you would not believe, though it were told you" (Habakkuk 1:5). Praise Him. I always thought of Pastor Chuck as Moses and now think of Pastor Brian as Joshua taking this generation to the promised land, waiting for a fresh pouring of the Spirit and lost in His love.
>
> I have been let go of my job. As you all know, I was written up, and the reason was that "sick people did not need to hear about Jesus and God." A week later I was let go. It

has been hard on me, and I am sure there is some spiritual warfare going on. Pray for me. It was a ministry I truly enjoyed, and I loved each one of those patients and cared deeply for their families. I worked there for about fourteen years and was blessed. God has done an amazing thing in my heart and is answering prayers to protect me from bitterness. My heart, Jesus' home. I am truly praying for anyone who wanted to see me go that their hearts will turn to the One who cares for their hearts. I am missing revealing Jesus and finding Jesus in every client I ministered to. The loss of health insurance and one salary is significant, even though my husband is capable of taking care of us. Praise God! My salary was mostly used to help others and for furthering the kingdom. But our God owns everything, and He is the One who gave and took away. Blessed be His name.

Well, I am waiting to see what God has for me in the next chapter of my life. I am contemplating volunteering. *God is good all the time . . .*

In His grip,
Maryama

* * * * *

Finding my bearings in this season was not easy. I went back and forth with forgiving. I knew in my heart that I needed to forgive the people who had let me go, yet even though in my heart I did, the stench of lies and injustice lingered in my soul. Some days were harder than others.

This started spilling over into my relationship with my Jesus and God's forgiveness toward me. If I had indeed been forgiven and brought into God's fold, how was it that I was struggling with unforgiveness toward people who had committed an offense against me? I sought God diligently regarding this matter and hung in there for about two months. I had a difficult time passing by the injustice and wanted God to do something about it. After all, I had been fired for His sake.

Again the sweetness of Jesus came through, and He asked me this question: "Did I forgive you because of justice or because of mercy? If because of mercy, why are you seeking justice for them and not mercy?" I became undone, and I wept much for my iniquities. I realized again His amazing love for this wicked heart of mine. I thanked Him for His incredible grace and mercy and said, "Lord, I am so sorry. I thank You for Your forgiveness through Your mercy. Lord Jesus, I do not have what it takes to forgive and also to bless them without You, but I am willing to walk this path with You. Only keep my heart and mind totally for You so that I can be healed."

That day I released those people to God. I started to pray for them, that they would side with God and not against Him and that His will would be done in their lives. Forgiveness came, and pain was reduced. Even though it surfaces once in a while, its power continues to diminish day by day.

I often think of the time when Peter asked Jesus how many times we must forgive. "Seven times?" he asked. And Jesus said, "Seven times seventy." Our Lord is smart—He knows that the offense we think was committed against us will surface over and over again. That's why He said seven times seventy. God is good all the time.

Forgiving and being forgiven is a lifelong issue. We get hurt, but we hurt others as well, so in order to forgive, we must first be secure in our own forgiveness from God. Only then can we be free to forgive. It is a journey. When we get hurt, having justice always comes up first, because we are created in God's image, and we tend to crave justice first rather than mercy. So we have to be reminded of God's mercy continuously and experience His unconditional forgiveness so that we can extend the same to others, knowing that they can do nothing to reverse the offense that was committed against us.

15
NEW OPPORTUNITIES
TO SERVE

O LORD my God, I cried out to You, and You healed me.
Psalm 30:2

With my chaplaincy ended, I began sowing the seeds of a new chapter in my life.

I attended an eight-week seminar on ministering to dementia patients, and afterward I applied for volunteer work in a hospice company. I began visiting three to four patients each week, and they became truly precious to me. Each one is different, and their unique personalities come out in ways that are uniquely theirs. I am truly blessed by them.

I love people with dementia, because they are extremely transparent. There is no fluff in their lives, and they do not have to pretend to impress others. I find them smart and beautiful.

I chose to minister to these people because they are the least visited. One reason for this is that it is impossible to have intellectual interaction with them. Since they don't remember or recognize anyone, people think that it does not matter if no one visits them, but nothing could be further from the truth. Since we approach life trying to please people, visiting can be a way of impressing others, but since people with dementia don't recognize others and therefore can't be impressed with us, it is easy for us to avoid visiting them.

Another reason that dementia patients are not visited much is that it is too painful for their families to see their loved one in this condition. And since these people don't have the capacity to build others' ego by loving them, it is in many cases no major loss to their family members not to visit. Sadly, all this is rooted in our perception of conditional love and conditional acceptance.

Whatever the case may be, I have the opportunity to visit and love these people unconditionally with the pure and unadulterated love of our precious Jesus. This is easy for me. Knowing the love of God helps me, as does having no history with them. I simply love them with no expectations—no straightening them out or correcting them. I am all in for the ride.

Some of the people I visit are in an infantile state, and I just sit with them and, with their permission through body language, gently stroke their foreheads. I make good eye contact with them and read to them and sing to them. I hum soothing sounds and share with them the words of life, encouraging them with the continuous reminder that they are beloved by me but most of all beloved by the God who spoke the universe into existence.

Some I take walks with, exploring their environment with them. We look at the flowers and the rocks and feel the sand. Or we look through their pictures, admiring the clothes they wore and how they looked beautiful. Some I play cards with, and they always "win." We laugh together, and I let them tell their stories over and over in their own terms. I visit each week, the same day every week and at almost the same time of day. They don't remember that I came before, and that makes a brand-new experience every time. I look forward to visiting them with true love and enjoyment. Jesus enjoys visiting them, and they enjoy Him as well. Jesus in me, the hope of glory (see Colossians 1:27).

People ask me if I get tired of visiting these patients. They think it is not rewarding, for the people do not even know that I am visiting them. I kindly answer, "But *I* know that I visit, and I have a hunch that they know also. But most of all, Someone else knows." I have a spiritual connection with them, so my visits to my precious patients continue to this day. When I visit, I experience Jesus in their presence, and I see Him in their eyes. Oh, the wonder of God, He is indeed expanding and getting bigger in my life! He manifests Himself everywhere, every day. I am astonished by Him. Who would have thought that I would find Him in the eyes of dementia patients?

As believers, God should become bigger in our lives, but sometimes as we grow in our faith, we make God smaller and put Him in a box. We follow formulas for how we think He is to function in our lives, and in the process He is reduced. May it not be so in our lives. He must remain the untamed lion of Judah, showing up whenever He wants, doing whatever He desires. Praise Him.

* * * * *

Another ministry that God brought into my life after I lost my job is encouraging young women. Some are married, some single.

If there has ever been a time when young women need guidance and encouragement in their marriages or relationships and to learn to be godly women in a challenging world, it is now. We, the women of the sixties, seventies, or even eighties, are the recipients of women's liberation, and we raised our daughters to be self-sufficient and to take care of themselves. While there is merit to this, sadly, our daughters have lost their tenderness. In trying to be equal with men, they lost their identity, which is tenderness, love, mercy, nurturing, nesting, protecting, and encouraging. They were told the lie that they should be equal with men, but they didn't realize that this actually reduced them.

Women are the finer sex. We have the capacity to endure the pain of childbirth and the discomfort of nurturing life in our bodies for nine months while we suffer morning sickness and hemorrhoids. We can manage two or three projects at one time. We have eyes in the backs of our heads—we see and hear our kids while involved in a deep conversation with a friend and at the same time preparing a meal. We are multifaceted, we are delicate yet resilient, we are good listeners, we are nurturers, we are builders, we are nesters, we are nurses and doctors, we are counselors and negotiators. We have empathy for others' pain; we cover others' mistakes and shortcomings. We are daughters, sisters, mothers, friends, and much more. And we want to be equal with men? Are we saying that God did not do a good job creating us?

Women's liberation has not been kind to us. Instead of taming and calming the savage behavior of men while at the same time encouraging the lion in them and fine-tuning them, we beat our men down and encourage them to explore their feminine side. Now they are full of estrogen, and we are full of testosterone. I don't know how it happened, but we switched sides—and yet we still expect men to be our knights in shining armor. Is it possible for a man who is beaten down and full of estrogen to be a woman's hero? I have never seen a man so beaten down as the American man. Everywhere we look, he has been stripped of his dignity and his leadership, and he is belittled and humiliated—yes, in our churches as well.

I see subtle evidence of this even among Christians, such as women driving their husbands. It looks innocent, but what does it tell a man about his leadership and his honor? Negative remarks that we make about our husbands, whether in their presence or absence, are equally damaging.

Christian women treat their husbands much better than the women in the world, and it should be so, but still we fall far below God's standards, and that is what counts. Not our standards but God's.

When I married Ken, I had to be secure in my relationship with God. That is the beginning of wisdom, because only Jesus can meet my need for love, acceptance, and a sense of belonging. Also, knowing that Ken is my brother has helped me to live a peaceful and quiet life with him. Truly my Kenny is a kind and gentle man who always, I believe, thinks of me first. But the fact is, I had to be safe and secure in the love of Jesus and to depend on Him for all my needs, because as good as my husband is, he fails me at times.

And without a doubt, I fail him. Yes, we have our issues, but when the flesh gets in the way, we recover quickly by giving each other space to process what happened and by listening to the gauge of the Holy Spirit. If the hurt is deeper, I take my case to my Abba and tell Him how I was mistreated. I narrate all the details. He is a good listener—He doesn't have to watch sports or play with His smartphone or listen to the news or keep an eye on the stock market. After He listens He never discusses Ken's issues with me but strengthens me and reassures me that all is well. Thus He prevents me from airing my husband's shortcomings. What a comfort! Not only that, but He gives me points on how to relate to my husband. I tell you, without Jesus our relationship would not have a chance. But being a godly wife is not hard when we are secure in *His* love.

When I mentor the young ladies, I listen first. Then I begin sharing with them from a counselor's best resources: the Word of God, the Holy Spirit, and personal life experience. I probe the young ladies' relationship with Jesus and point out to them how Jesus sees them: beautiful, beloved, and adored by Him. I touch on the issue of pride, which is really none other than insecurity. And I encourage the ladies to learn to enjoy Jesus, because when they do, they will enjoy their husbands. After all, they and their husbands are one in Christ. I remind them that their husbands are also their brothers and that they will be in heaven together, so resolving issues here on earth is a good thing to do.

I also teach the young ladies how to communicate with their husbands. It helps to avoid ambiguous conversation and to make it clear to their husbands, in truth and tenderness, what they want to convey. I encourage them to avoid discussing major issues when their husbands are watching sports or when they are hungry. I tell them to try to set a time to talk about issues so that their husbands may prepare themselves and pray for wisdom and tenderness toward their wives. Also, it is hard for men to multitask, so I teach them that it is best to stick to one issue at a time. One last bit of helpful advice: if the ladies get engaged in their husbands' games, it shows the men that their wives are interested in them.

Just as Jesus does with me, I never discuss their husbands with them except to build the husbands up. The world is already beating them up; it does not need my help. The language of love is grace.

So, beloved sisters, let us build up our husbands and encourage them to take their place in the world, in the church, and in our homes. Instead of asking our husbands to pay attention to us after they have worked all day, draw them in instead. We are women—we have the tools to draw our men in. Believe me, our husbands are not complicated.

Kay Smith, Pastor Chuck's wife, used to tell women to sizzle some onion and garlic before their husbands come home, even if they haven't thought of what they are going to cook. When he arrives home, they should smile, give him a hug and a kiss, and ask him how his day went. This goes a long way and may save a marriage. Only God can fix our marriages and our relationships. We must lean on Him for wisdom.

We women have been deceived and lied to long enough by the culture. Let's go back and build our homes by building our men, and let's turn our eyes from the world, which is truly committed to destroying our marriages and our men.

I have the privilege of knowing many young women who want to do right in their marriages and to love their husbands but who lack the raw material to strengthen and build their homes. Even though they are believers and have heard and read the Word, they do not apply it to their lives on a daily basis. We all fail in this. We hear the Word but do not let it come into our hearts and own it as life.

The Word of God is life, and it gives life. I encourage the young women to know that the only person they can change is themselves, through Jesus. I hear how their husbands are failing them, and what I learn about how far the culture has fallen breaks my heart. But I never focus on what the women's husbands are doing wrong—I simply tell the young ladies to pray for them. I allow my Jesus to speak through me, giving me wisdom to strengthen and build these women and to teach them the foundation of Scripture.

And I encourage them that life is an adventure. We are to enjoy God in the good times and also when we go through difficulties. For the adventure of life is to learn. The nature of life is to change. The goal of life is to grow. The beauty of life is to give. The essence of life is to care. The joy of life is to love. Only when we are willing to learn, to change, to grow, to give, to care, to love can we truly experience God.

Christian women, build your home, and honor your husbands. Christian men, love your wives, and learn to lead with velvet hands and the heart of a lion.

Dear Lord Jesus, our girls have been deceived by feminism, and our boys have been beaten down by feminism. May they embrace who You have made them to be and enjoy each other's strengths and cover each other's weaknesses.

* * * * *

I have been amazingly blessed to minister to and visit my sweet dementia patients and also to mentor young ladies through the love of my Jesus and to encourage them in their faith walk. Both groups are a blessing to me, as I learn from them as well. I love them.

When I lost my job as a hospice chaplain, a Christian sister, trying to comfort me, quoted Romans 8:28 to me. At that time a hug or a touch on the shoulder would have been more comforting to me, but I am happy to say that Romans 8:28 is alive and well in my heart, because I have seen and tasted the goodness of God in my loss. Indeed, all things do work together for good for those who love God and are called according to His purpose.

God never takes something good away from His children unless He intends to replace it with something better in our lives. When I was a chaplain, I focused on the sick, and while this was profitable and rewarding, looking back I see how it had become routine. Fatigue was settling in, and I was in danger of losing the awe! I once ministered to the sick and shared my resource with others, but now God is telling me, "Share yourself with My people and with the world around you."

Our God is unchangeable—the immutable God. His truth stays the same. But His work is ever changing; He makes things new every day and helps me to see things in different ways. He is dynamic; He is alive; He is vibrant and energetic. He grows us through the ups and downs of life, and He desires His children to be forever evolving upward, growing in His grace. He wants us to be rivers of living water instead of stagnant ponds. I was obedient when living with Him as a chaplain, but He wanted me to come up higher, and in order to draw me near to Him, He stepped back a little so that I could desire Him more. He is dancing with me. How glorious!

I am grateful to my God, the Lord Jesus, for bringing me to where I am, and equally thankful for all the people He used to bring me to this restful, exciting place—even those who wished me harm.

I long to experience God and express His love. Trials help me to know God more deeply, and even though I am not in a hurry to ask God for more trials, I have been blessed by the ones I've had. When future ones come—and they will—I am confident that He will see me through. Oh, the blessing of knowing God's faithfulness! In all our trials and tribulations, He remains faithful.

16
REJOICING IN JESUS IN EVERY SEASON

I will sing to the LORD, because He has dealt bountifully with me.
Psalm 13:6

It is somewhat ironic that I chose Psalm 13:6 for this chapter, because as I write, I am in the middle of great pain and trial. Even though the love of Jesus is comfortable, I am also learning that there is sometimes difficulty in being comfortable with Him.

You see, He is beckoning me to come closer—to step out of my comfortable place and to follow Him in new ways. And I am afraid, for He is stirring up my comfortable nest and calling me to ministry that I've never done before. I'm not sure exactly what He wants from me—I only know that the path ahead is new and different. My Lord is stepping backward a little, and He wants me to pursue Him, but He is leading me into unfamiliar territory, and He seems to be in the dark.

In this tremendous trial, He seems quiet. But He is telling me to love Him. I am confused by this, because I thought I loved Him already. Is He asking me to love Him on a different level? I am stunned, for I don't know how to do as He asks, so I get closer and ask Him to teach me to pray for this extraordinary love. He reveals to me that the reason I am afraid to get closer is that I don't want to be consumed by Him, for if He consumes me, I will have nothing left for self.

Prayer. I am asking Him to forgive me for spending so much time pretending to know Him, because I will never know Him as He is known until that glorious day when I enter eternity. But now He is stripping me down and exposing my heart with love so severe that His wounds are healing me.

I love being a Christian, because we never arrive at our destination until our last breath, and so we yearn for Him day by day. I am not sure what will come of this trial that I am in or the many trials that will come my way in this life, but I know who holds my trials. I know that my Redeemer lives, and though He may slay me, yet I will trust Him (see Job 19:25; 13:15). In this tough place I am seeking Him and His knowledge, for the glory of the Lord is to conceal knowledge, and the power of the king is to search it out (see Proverbs 25:2).

* * * * *

Another burden on my heart during this season of trial is my daughter's spiritual welfare. When Ken and I first came to Calvary Chapel Costa Mesa, I had the privilege of sharing my testimony with Cheryl Brodersen, and I also told her of my concern for my beloved prodigal. Cheryl introduced me to a ministry in our church called the prodigal ministry, which I immediately joined. What I found was a pot of gold refined in the fire. I became part of this group of godly women who prayed and interceded for their prodigals, standing in the gap for them and waiting patiently for God to act on their behalf.

When I was first saved, Eda was kind and respectful to go to church with me, but as she got older, she moved further and further from the faith. Maybe it was because of the teaching we were receiving; perhaps she thought that she could not measure up. And who could?

She remarks now that the happiest time she remembers is before I was a Christian. No one will ever know how deeply that hurts, and I take the blame of my daughter not being a Christian. God has forgiven me, and so has my daughter, but I have difficulty forgiving myself. Of all the offenses I committed, this is the hardest, because I was not diligent to teach my daughter how beautiful Jesus is.

It has been a long road, but God is redeeming our relationship one day at a time, and love is abounding. I know that she will come back to her own border according to His perfect will and for His glory. God's universal grace and my prayers, with my sisters in the prodigal ministry, are keeping her afloat.

For several years I have met with the ladies in this ministry once a week to pray and to share, and we find ourselves being purified and made stronger in the Lord. As we grow in His grace together, we learn more about God, and we mature to love Him and each other more. The cross once again comes into view—loving God, loving people. Here we are, a group of women gathering to intercede for our prodigals, and God is changing *our* hearts toward Him and toward our children. He is teaching us to love our prodigals unconditionally, as He does.

With these women I have cultivated a friendship, a sisterhood, a bond that is unbreakable, because this bond is none other than our Lord Jesus Christ. We are strengthened through sharing with each other what the Lord is showing each one of us.

Our prodigals come with all kinds of issues. Some are homeless, some are on drugs or alcohol, some have issues with the law, some are well educated and doing well in life with professions of every sort, but they all have several things in common: Jesus is missing them, His arms are open wide to embrace them, and godly women are kneeling before Jesus on their behalf. We trust God to redeem our sons and daughters, and we believe for what God can do in their lives.

It is at times arduous, but we wait patiently for God to hear our prayers and to act on behalf of our sons and daughters. I am expectantly waiting for the Lord for my loved ones' salvation, for I am persuaded that this is His heart's desire as well.

In the meantime, I am deeply thankful for His universal grace that shines upon the believer and the unbeliever alike.

Our children simply don't have what it takes to come to Him—Jesus is the only One who can draw them to Himself. We were in the same predicament once, and by His grace God saved us. He is teaching us to be gracious toward our children with the patience and tender mercies He has shown us.

We thought He could change our prodigals, but indeed He is changing us.

Our leader's words of hope and encouragement are healing us. Each week she shares with us a verse from the Bible, and we meditate on it as we seek God's face that week. I am truly thankful for my Jesus and for this godly woman and the rest of the sisters who stand by me. Without them my journey would have been unbearable.

The Bible is full of the promises of God, but several verses have been especially profitable to us:

> Trust in the LORD with all your heart, and lean not on your own understanding; in all your ways acknowledge Him, and He shall direct your paths. (Proverbs 3:5–6)

> I will heal their backsliding, I will love them freely, for My anger has turned away from him. (Hosea 14:4)

> I know the thoughts that I think toward you, says the LORD, thoughts of peace and not of evil, to give you a future and a hope. Then you will call upon Me and go and pray to Me, and I will listen to you. And you will

seek Me and find Me, when you search for Me with all your heart. (Jeremiah 29:11–13)

The LORD has appeared of old to me, saying: "Yes, I have loved you with an everlasting love; therefore with lovingkindness I have drawn you." (Jeremiah 31:3)

Thus says the LORD: "Refrain your voice from weeping, and your eyes from tears; for your work shall be rewarded, says the LORD, and they shall come back from the land of the enemy. There is hope in your future, says the LORD, that your children shall come back to their own border." (Jeremiah 31:16–17)

Fear not, for I am with you; be not dismayed, for I am your God. I will strengthen you, yes, I will help you, I will uphold you with My righteous right hand. (Isaiah 41:10)

Through these and many other promises, our Lord reminds us that He hears our prayers and desires to save our prodigals. Whether we see them saved in this life, or whether they will be saved after we have gone to the life after, only He knows, but we desire to see them saved while we are here on earth. So we are sustained and comforted by God, and we encourage each other in this truth and never give up.

I imagine that God gives us grandchildren to give us a second chance. Ken and I were blessed to become grandparents in 2013. We adore Heather, and she adores us. She makes me feel young, and seeing the world through her eyes is beautiful. I held her a few hours after she was born, and her grandpa and I dedicated her to the Lord. We blessed her parents and prayed that they would have wisdom to raise her to the light.

* * * * *

In this unsettling season God is reminding me, as He has done over and over, of the same simple lesson: I am not to do great things for Him but to let Him do great things through me. I must abide in Him. I struggled with busyness when I became an American Christian, but God insists that the only thing that has any value is what He has already done and what He can do in my life for His glory.

Being overly busy for God is a sure way to lose the joy of the Lord. There is nothing wrong with serving in itself, but service has a tendency to encourage pride in me, as if I were doing something for God. But Jesus said that He is the vine and I am a branch, and it is the vine that does the work. So my Lord wants to serve through me.

I have to be on guard and make sure that I stay dependent on God for everything, because self, Satan, and the world feed on my pride. My struggle with the flesh will be with me to the end, but sin cannot overcome me as long as I abide in Christ. So I stay in the vine by His grace (see John 15:4).

When we abide in the vine, we flourish. We are vibrant and happy, and we are free from fear or worry. We are continuously filled with the Spirit of Christ. The affairs of this world and the schemes of Satan, who relentlessly tries to separate us from the vine, are destroyed. Satan's purpose is to steal, kill, and destroy, but our beloved Savior came that we may have life more abundantly (see John 10:10). Jesus wants us to be in His presence and experience Him in childlike delight, savoring His every blessing and proclaiming Him to a watching world.

Abiding in Jesus means relying on Him for everything. Just as a branch cannot survive without the vine, so I cannot survive without Jesus. As I abide in Him, I simply become a fruit bearer—not working, just producing fruit and praying that He will produce much more fruit in me. It's truly glorious.

* * * * *

God's progressive revelation of Himself in my life has been truly amazing. My flesh gets in the way, but God faithfully and gently reminds me that I had nothing to do with His salvation—instead He who began a good work in me will be faithful to complete it (see Philippians 1:6).

His ultimate purpose is for me to know Him. I get to know Him, as I have from the beginning, by exploring His Word. Then I apply what I learn to my daily walk. As I walk with Jesus and become comfortable with Him and His love for me, trials come, and my knowledge of Him is tested. So I examine what I have learned about Him to find out if I have fostered any false information, and as the Word and the Spirit clear up any misunderstandings, God reveals more of Himself to me. I experience more clarity of mind and heart, and my love for Him grows.

The Bible is the manual for every aspect of life. Every condition or situation is addressed in it. The Word of God is a life-giving book—it has power to change us. It is instructional, it is historical, it is poetic, it is prophetic, and it is the gospel—the good news. The Old Testament is the New Testament concealed, and the New Testament is the Old Testament revealed. It is rich. I love reading it.

From the beginning to the end, the Bible is the story of Jesus.

The first two chapters of Genesis show God's absolutely perfect creation. Then in chapter 3, we read of paradise lost—man and God were disconnected, and perpetual sacrifice began. The rest of the Bible narrates a sad story of broken men without God and God's undying love for them. It's a story full of tears, agony, and death. God is as passionate for mankind as a mother seeking her lost child and a father waiting for his prodigal to return.

Our Lord is the great I AM, the self-existent One, the eternal Being. He is all that man ever needed. In Genesis He is the provider. In Exodus He is the healer. In Judges He is our peace. In Psalms He is our shepherd. In Jeremiah He is righteousness.

In the Gospels I find that Jesus is the light of the world (see John 8:12). He is the way, the truth, and the life (see John 14:6). Then a heavy price was paid—God sacrificed Himself for us. But Jesus is the resurrection and the life—death was defeated (see John 11:25)! He bridged the gap between man and God. Because of the resurrection we have forgiveness from the past, power for the present, and hope for the future. The resurrection of Jesus is the cornerstone of the Christian faith.

The last two chapters of the Bible tell us of paradise recovered, when God and man will be fully connected: "God will wipe away every tear from their eyes; there shall be no more death, nor sorrow, nor crying. There shall be no more pain, for the former things have passed away" (Revelation 21:4). Selah.

Our God is the Alpha and the Omega, the Beginning and the End, the First and the Last. He is the Root and Offspring of David. He is the holy Lord God Almighty, who was and is and is to come. He is immense, omnipotent, omniscient, omnipresent, immortal, immutable, a holy God. The universe bears witness to Him and His creation. This God who yearned for man throughout the Scriptures still yearns for every one of us with His hands wide open to receive us the moment we respond. Oh God, what are we that You are mindful of us? (See Psalm 8:4.)

Jesus Christ is God's perfect plan to redeem us and to connect us back to God. To the unbelieving world, Christianity makes no sense, because Christians lose everything to gain Christ. But remember, the world doesn't understand that we possess everything. We are cast down but not conquered: "We are hard-pressed on every side, yet not crushed; we are perplexed, but not in despair; persecuted, but not forsaken; struck down, but not destroyed" (2 Corinthians 4:8–9). Jesus shines in our hearts to show His love, mercy, and grace and to persuade a perishing and unbelieving world that He is the only hope against darkness.

Getting to know God is the greatest privilege I have experienced and will ever experience. In this season of my life, as God is training me to know Him more through trials, I am finding Him in His Word, the book of living water. I am blessed as well to have a church that teaches the Word of God, precept upon precept, with tender, loving care and grace. Our pastor is a faithful shepherd who leads the congregation to the greatest Shepherd of all—our Lord and Savior Jesus Christ. Through the Word of God, I am learning and drawing near to Him.

God is good all the time, and He is the rewarder of all who seek Him (see Hebrews 11:6).

> [May] the God of our Lord Jesus Christ, the Father of glory, . . . give to you the spirit of wisdom and revelation in the knowledge of Him, the eyes of your understanding being enlightened; that you may know what is the hope of His calling, what are the riches of the glory of His inheritance in the saints, and what is the exceeding greatness of His power toward us who believe, according to the working of His mighty power which He worked in Christ when He raised Him from the dead and seated Him at His right hand in the heavenly places, far above all principality and power and might and dominion, and every name that is named, not only in this age but also in that which is to come.

And He put all things under His feet, and gave Him to be head over all things to the church, which is His body, the fullness of Him who fills all in all. (Ephesians 1:17–23)

Amen.

AFTERWORD
CHANNELS OF HIS LOVE

*Love . . . bears all things, believes all things,
hopes all things, endures all things.*
1 Corinthians 13:4, 7

As a young Christian, I knew nothing of God, but Jesus showed up in every area of my life. He was kind and tender. He heard me when I talked to Him, and He spoke to me through His Word, through quiet time, through prayer. I learned that prayer is not a set of rituals but simply talking to God about anything and learning to hear what He has to say. It was beautiful.

As I grew in my faith over the years, I faced a number of struggles—a battle with legalism, rejection by my family, my husband's cancer and my Bell's palsy, my relationship with my daughter, my pastor's death, the loss of a much loved job. But in all these things I found again and again that Jesus alone was all I needed. It is never Jesus plus something. Jesus Himself is enough.

Psalm 45 is called "A Song of Love." It is about Jesus, the King, and His bride. In verses 10–11 it says,

> Listen, O daughter, consider and incline your ear; forget your own people also, and your father's house; so the King will greatly desire your beauty; because He is your Lord, worship Him.

When I read that, I realized that if I had stayed with my people and my father's house, the King would not have desired me, because I would not have been beautiful. He is the One who made me beautiful. In Him I was cleansed and purified. He took away my robe of covetousness and gave me a new robe—the robe of righteousness: "The royal daughter is all glorious within the palace; her clothing is woven with gold. She shall be brought to the King in robes of many colors" (Psalm 45:13–14).

This speaks of the Messiah and His bride—the church in which I am a member. Is this not awesome!

I have lost many things, but in Jesus I have gained everything.

As one of His precious children, He asks me, as He asks you, to be a partaker of His plan for all people to know Jesus. Jesus has made us participants in the riches of heaven here on earth so that we can illuminate and reveal Him in the world. He is the light, and we are His light bearers. Since Jesus is in us, we reflect His light to a dark world. The more the darkness increases, the light increases much more.

God wants those of us who know Him to express Him in a world full of pain, poverty, racism, war, famine, injustice, insecurity, and distrust. He is not asking us to change the world but to be instruments that *He* uses to change the world. We are to be channels of His love to bring peace, calm, sanity, and order wherever we go. We are called to promote peace with God, with self, with family, with neighbors, with the world, for our God is the author of peace.

God asks us to bless people with our words and deeds, to serve them, to meet their needs whenever we can through words of hope and encouragement. As we grow in grace, we begin to see the world around us with different eyes and to be more perceptive of people and their needs. Instead of being interesting, I am learning how to be interested in others. It is not easy for me to see people's pain, but it helps me when I remember that it is even harder for our Lord. I would rather feel people's pain than be indifferent, for it is not in the heart of Jesus to be indifferent.

At times I see darkness in people's lives—even those who seem to have it all together. One morning as I ran, I passed a lady who had the most frightening eyes I have ever seen. I tried to say good morning, but I was unable to speak, and as she passed me, the hair on my back stood up. Immediately I uttered the name of Jesus, and I was okay. This is one of the many times when I have realized that there is evil in the world. I prayed for this woman to be released.

In Jeremiah 29:7 our Lord says to "seek the peace of the city . . . and pray to the LORD for it; for in its peace you will have peace." How marvelous it is to be channels of peace and vessels that contain God. Glorious!

We are saved to bless, to serve, and to minister—it is in the Christian's DNA to care and to love. As I journey through this temporary life, I ask God to make me His light bearer each day. When I was touched by my Jesus, He healed my spiritual vision. He gave me focus and clarity both in the material world and in the spiritual world. His Spirit bears witness to my spirit regarding the things of God, and He allows me to see darkness so that as a light bearer I can shine the light on it and, wherever I am, cause the darkness to dissipate. Where there is light, there is no darkness.

We are disciples of Christ—that's our identity. Our Jesus is the light of the world, and we are His light bearers.

Oh Lord, walk with us in the garden of our hearts, where You have permanent residence. Thank You, Jesus, for pouring Your light into us so that we can be a beacon to others to reflect Your glory. Fill us with Your agape love, that we would seek the wellbeing of others unselfishly and unconditionally. Amen.

48012494R00117

Made in the USA
Charleston, SC
22 October 2015